# Ron Burgundy
## LET ME OFF AT THE TOP!
### MY CLASSY LIFE & OTHER MUSINGS

# Ron Burgundy
# *LET ME OFF AT THE TOP!*
## MY CLASSY LIFE & OTHER MUSINGS

CENTURY

Published by Century 2013

2 4 6 8 10 9 7 5 3 1

Book design by Elizabeth Rendfleisch
Illustration on page 154 by Fred Haynes
Photography credits appear on page 224
Jacket design by Michael Nagin
Jacket photographs: Emily Shur, TM & © Par. Pics. All rights reserved
(front and author); TM & © Par. Pics. All rights reserved (spine)

First published in Great Britain in 2013 by
Century
Random House, 20 Vauxhall Bridge Road,
London SW1V 2SA

www.randomhouse.co.uk

Addresses for companies within The Random House Group Limited can be found at:
www.randomhouse.co.uk

The Random House Group Limited Reg. No. 954009

A CIP catalogue record for this book
is available from the British Library

ISBN 9781780892245

The Random House Group Limited supports the Forest Stewardship
Council® (FSC®), the leading international forest-certification organisation.
Our books carrying the FSC label are printed on FSC®-certified paper.
FSC is the only forest-certification scheme supported by the leading
environmental organisations, including Greenpeace. Our paper procurement
policy can be found at: www.randomhouse.co.uk/environment

Printed and bound by Clays Ltd, St Ives Plc

# DISCLAIMER

Every word in this book is true. You can fact-check most of it but much of it lives within my brain. Fortunately for you my memory is infallible. With the exception of people, places, situations and dialogue, I'm like a walking encyclopedia of facts. You might as well chisel this baby in stone, because what you are holding is a perfect unchallengeable chronicle of American history and personal narrative. You are welcome.

# AUTHOR'S NOTE

It took me eight years to write this book. The research alone—fact-checking, reading the source materials, asking questions—was endless and I didn't care for it that much. I just didn't. But I persisted because I knew what I was doing was truly very important. A book is never the work of one man. Many people contribute to its failure, or as in this case, its success. Dorathoy Roberts at the Harvard Widener Library was instrumental in recovering so many facts and nautical terms. Janart Prancer aided my work immensely with her near-encyclopedic understanding of rare manuscripts in the Herzog August Library, Wolfenbüttel, Germany. Esther Nausbaum, head librarian at the prestigious Kirkland School of Dinosaurs, was instrumental in tracking down indispensable paleoecological records for chapter 15 in this book. Herb Kolowsky was ever watchful and patient, reading over many drafts of the manuscript as well as cleaning my gutters. I consulted with my dear friend and lover Doris Kearns Goodwin over many breakfasts in bed. Her sharp intellect and sharper teeth found their way into practically every page. Although we are no longer lovers because I don't know why, her knowledge of presidential history is the basis for chapter 12. Her dogged enthusiasm for the project was only outpaced by her enthusiasm for lovemaking, which I could barely equal. I don't know what to say about Doris really except if she's still out there and she would like another bounce, I would be game. Johnny Bench was an invaluable spell-checker. Lars Mankike brought an artistic eye to the project and a kind of European nihilism that was completely unnecessary. We fought often and he got what he deserved, so I'm not even sure why I'm thanking him here, but it's too late now. Sandy Duncan is full of boundless energy. What can I say about Veronica Corningstone, the love of my life? We've had our ups and downs for sure, and usually the downs were because of something stupid she said or did while losing blood. You really can't fault women for being irrational. Blood drips out of them willy-nilly and there's nothing they can do about it. It's like being a hemophiliac. I suspect science will one day cure them of this blood-dripping disease but until then, *Vive la différence.* Finally Baxter, my dog and best friend, saw me through many tough hours as I struggled with my emotions during this project. His love and support sustained me through extremely difficult excavations into my past. Only Baxter knows the pain I have lived. Our nightly talks formed the basis for what you hold in your hand now.

# WHY WRITE THIS BOOK?

Does mankind really need another book dumped onto the giant garbage heap of books already out there? Is there some pressing desire for the wisdom of a humble News Anchor in this world? Will it add to the great literary achievements throughout time or will it be lost in a swamp of trivial scribbling like pornography—devoured and then destroyed out of shame? I stand here (I write standing up) and I say, "No!" No, this book will NOT be lost! This book is necessary. It's an important work from an important man. I was the number one News Anchor in all of San Diego. My name is Ron Burgundy and what you have in your hands is a very big deal. It's . . . my . . . life. It's my words. It's my gift to you.

If the truth be told, I've wanted to write a book for a long time, but how? How do you write a book? Oh sure, I know you get paper and pencils and make yourself a pot of coffee and you stay up all night and write one. Seems simple enough, but it's not. There's a very long tradition of book writing going back through history all the way to Roman times, and if you know history like I do you understand that book writing is NOT EASY! Rule number one sayeth the bard, "To thy own self be truthful in regards to yourself." I knew from the beginning, before even purchasing the paper and the pencils and the cans of coffee, I would have to spend a little time getting to know me. I've been so busy being Ron Burgundy the legend that I never stopped to really get to know Ron Burgundy the man. Before I wrote one word of this masterpiece I took long walks through the streets of San Diego trying to make friends with a guy I barely knew: myself. I talked to myself, that's right, in bars, at bus stops, in laundromats, wherever my muse took me. I recommend it. Go out and talk to yourself. Record the conversations like I did. I had a small lightweight twenty-pound Grundig reel-to-reel tape recorder with a built-in microphone. A typical conversation went like this:

**Ron**
**Hey, good friend of mine.**

**Ron**
**Hey right back at you.**

**Ron**
**What's it all about?**

**Ron**

It's a good question, Ron. You ask tough questions.

**Ron**

It's my business, I'm a News Anchor by trade.

**Ron**

No kidding, that's important!

**Ron**

Yeah, it's really nothing. I'm kind of a big deal around San Diego.

**Ron**

It sounds damn impressive.

**Ron**

It is in a way. It's pretty impressive. Are you hungry?

**Ron**

I could definitely go for some fish-and-chips. Do you know where they have the best fish-and-chips in San Diego?

**Ron**

I do. There's a one-of-a-kind sea shanty called Long John Silver's that fixes up delicious fish-and-chips at a reasonable price.

**Ron**

Man, that sounds yummy.

**Ron**

Why don't you join me? I'm heading over there now.

**Ron**

How far of a walk is it?

**Ron**

About six miles.

**Ron**

Do you want to discuss life some more while we walk?

**Ron**

No, let's shut it down until after we eat.


Night after night like a ghost I walked the streets of San Diego holding conversations with only myself. Sometimes the conversations were trivial, like the time I got into an argument over which dog breed, Labrador or collie, was better at learning tricks, but sometimes they reached a sublime level of deep thinking, like this conversation I recorded while sitting on a transit bus.


**Ron**

What's it all mean, Ron?

**Ron**

Sometimes I think we're all crazy.

**Ron**

I know what you mean. I feel crazy myself sometimes.

**Ron**

I mean, what's to stop me from lighting this bus on fire?

**Ron**

I know! But keep your voice down, okay?

**Ron**

I mean it! There's nothing. What holds us together, Ron? Very little. VERY LITTLE!

**Ron**

Ron, you're in your head too much. Breathe.

**Ron**

No but listen to me, Ron, the world is made of strands of particles and atoms that commingle without meaning, taking form momentarily, decaying, finding new form— senseless activity without a guiding center. How can we make sense of it? Burning down this bus with all these people holds the same value as giving birth to a child. Don't you get it?

**Ron**

Keep it together, buddy.

**Ron**

I WILL NOT BE TALKED TO IN THIS WAY. I AM NOT A CHILD! I MIGHT JUST BURN DOWN THIS BUS TO PROVE A POINT!

**Bus Driver**

Do we have a problem?

**Ron**

Cool it, Ron. You're making people nervous.

**Ron**

**I DON'T CARE! I DON'T CARE! I'M GOING TO BURN DOWN THIS BUS!**

**Unidentified Male Voice**
**Get him. Hold him down.**

**Ron**

**I'M RON BURGUNDY! Ow, come on. CHANNEL FOUR NEWS!**

**Ron**

**He's okay. Stop hitting. He's okay . . . he's okay, let him breathe.**

I have over a thousand hours of recorded conversations with myself. What was I looking for? What was I trying to get at? I knew if I was going to write a book I would have to call on all of my powers of concentration. I would have to dig deep into the man, not the myth but the man, Ron Burgundy. To begin with I climbed Mount San Gorgonio, the highest peak in all of Southern California, and I called on an old friend, mighty Athena, the goddess of wisdom and courage, to guide me in this noble endeavor.

There I stood naked to the stars and the great gods above and yelled out, "My name is Ron Burgundy and I call on you, Athena, for inspiration! I am going to write a book. It shall be the story of my life, a great novel! I'm not sure *novel* is what you call a life story. There's another name for *life story* and I have forgotten it. For it does not matter! Brobalia! It's called a Brobalia! No, that's not it but it starts with a *B*. It is of no importance, mighty Athena! I stand here alone, naked on this mount with these tourists from Germany"—it's true, there were some tourists from Germany up there as well—"to ask for your guidance and wisdom while writing this Binocular. Nope, that's a word for something different. NO MATTER! Bisojagular! Still not right but I'm getting closer, fair Athena, and thanks for your patience—let all the gods know, Zeus, Apollo, Poseidon and Hestia, to name only a few, that I will ask for their strength in writing this Braknopod. Way off! My old pal Doris Kearns Goodwin would surely know the name you give a life story. She was a real egghead, among other things. Anyway, Athena, just help me write this thing. I swear to you that I will remember the name people give to life stories the minute I get down from this mountain! Thank you, brave Athena!"

Judging by what I have written here I can say with all confidence she heard my plaintive cries that raw night up on that tourist trap of a peak in the San Bernardino Mountains.

Now, I'm not going to lie, a searching evaluation of who I am has been an ordeal, not just for me but for those closest to me. It's been hard on my wife, Veronica, and Baxter, my dog, and for anyone who lives within screaming distance of my house and for law enforcement personnel. I went all in on this quest for self-discovery. William Thackeray Thoreau once said, "Desperate men lead lives of quiet songs that are left unsung when they do end up in their cold tombs." Something like that. Anyway, the point is you only go around once and you really need to go for the gold!

I can tell you this: There were a lot of people out there

who didn't think it was such a good idea to write a book. I know stuff about certain people and let's just say that sometimes knowledge can be dangerous. When word got out I was writing a "tell-all" book there were attempts made on my life! This is serious business. Most men would have run for the hills. Not me; I welcome the challenge. There is a chance I may have to go into hiding after this book comes out. I can't say where I will disappear to but more than likely it will be my cabin I purchased with George C. Scott's cousin. Its location can never be known. Scott's cousin is never there and it's less rustic than you think, with a pool table and full bar as well as a washer-dryer combo, and it's within walking distance to the Big Bear Lake general store.

Death threats are an occupational hazard of course for us anchormen. I'm very comfortable living each minute with the expectation of being attacked. It's been many years since JFK told me he used to enjoy Marilyn Monroe from behind while Joe DiMaggio looked on in the corner. The main players have all left the stage, so perhaps now is the time to speak out without fear of reprisal. Maybe telling the truth is more important than any danger I may face. Then again, maybe the truth has nothing to do with it. Maybe I just don't like it when people say, "Ron, you can't write a book, you don't have the courage," or "Ron, you can't write a book, you don't know how to type," or "Ron, have you ever even read a book?" It's the naysayers who get me. I like surprising people. I always have. I think everyone in the world took it for granted that I would not have the balls to write this book. I've got the balls, big hairy misshapen balls in a wrinkly sack. This book is a testament to my giant balls. If you want some feel-good story about how to live your life, then go look elsewhere. This book is a hard-hitting, no-holds-barred, unafraid account of my exceptional life with some words of wisdom thrown in for good measure. You won't find a lot of fluff here. If you're looking for fluff to take to the beach, check out the Holy Bible. This ain't that book.

So who am I? That's what this book is about. Over the next eight hundred pages (unless some bitch of an editor gets ahold of it with his clammy hands and snotty nose) I will let you in on a very big secret: my life. Of course some of it isn't such a secret. Some of it you know already. I'm a man. A News Anchor. A lover. Husband. A friend to animals on land and at sea. A handsome devil. A connoisseur of fine wine. I have one of the classiest collections of driftwood art in the world. I can throw a Wham-O Frisbee if I have to, but I prefer not to. I love the outdoors. Nature drives me nuts. I make pancakes for anyone who asks. I take long nude walks on the beach. I play jazz flute, not for business but for pleasure. I'm a world-class water-ski instructor. I don't care a lick about the fashion world, although they seem to care an awful lot about me. My best friend is a dog named Baxter. I'm quite famous. I'm a history buff. I collect authentic replications of Spanish broadswords. I smoke a pipe on occasion, not for profit but for pleasure. I've been known to sing out loud at weddings and funerals. I'm a collector of puns. I have over three hundred handcrafted shoes of all sizes. I don't give a damn about broccoli. I believe all men have the right to self-pleasure. I carry a picture of Buffy Sainte-Marie in my wallet and I'm not even Catholic. My favorite drink is scotch. My second-favorite drink is a Hairy Gaylord. I'm affiliated with at least a hundred secret societies; some of them, like the Knights of Thunder, will kill you just for printing their name. I adore tits. I will never be persuaded to try yogurt. I'm allergic to fear. Other men have fallen in love with me in a sexual way and that's okay. I have mixed feelings about bicycles. My handmade fishing lures are sought after by fly-fishermen the world over. I've never been one for blue jeans. Sandals on another man have been known to make me vomit. My Indian name is Ketsoh Silaago. My French name is Pierre Laflume. I can never tell anyone about what happened in Youngstown, Ohio, one January night. There are no other people who look like me on this planet; I've looked. Babies, bless their souls, give me the creeps. I own a chain of hobby stores in the Twin Cities I have never seen. I once ate a ham dinner and then realized it was not ham. People tell me I look like Mickey Rooney. Woody the Woodpecker cracks me up every time. That's the basic stuff; now prepare yourself for the journey—the journey into an extraordinary life.

# THE BOY FROM HAGGLEWORTH

The story we were told as children went something like this. . . . On June 27, 1844, Joseph Smith, the great Mormon martyr, and his brother Hyrum were killed by a mob in Carthage, Illinois. In the middle of the mob was a smooth opportunist named Franklin Haggleworth. Haggleworth was on his way to Keokuk, Iowa, and the Mississippi River to cheat people out of money. As the mob grew outside the jail where Smith and his brother were held, Haggleworth stirred up the crowd with anti-Mormon slogans and songs. Up to that point the crowd had been a peaceful assembly of reasonable people willing to discuss whether Smith or his brother had transgressed any laws. Haggleworth saw an opening. With his honey-tongued skill for oratory he was able to cajole the law-abiding citizenry into a frenzied pack of murderers. Within minutes of his opening his mouth, the crowd stormed the jail and shot the two brothers. Haggleworth ran off to the Mormon camp to report the sad news that their leader had been shot. Feigning sympathy with the now-distraught Mormons, he produced a dirty dinner plate and proclaimed Joseph Smith himself had given it to him right before his death. According to Haggleworth it was the last plate given to Smith by the angel Moroni. But unlike the plates Smith "translated," this new plate had never been translated. Pretending to read the plate, a fairly crappy piece of pottery that sits in the Haggleworth Museum to this day, he told the crowd that a new religion would be born out of Mormonism—a new religion dedicated to worshipping the penis of Mr. Franklin Haggleworth. He went on to explain that this new religion required up to twelve but no less than three women "who didn't have to be virgins because that seemed kind of overused" to frequently see to the needs of his ever-demanding penis. For the most part the men and women in the Mormon settlement were not convinced of Haggleworth's "vision." But try and remember—this was a strange part of American history and folks were dropping everything to follow men with heaven-born plates. There were nudist colonies and polygamist silver-ware-making colonies and people going to séances left and right—not like now, when reason holds sway. This was a wildly superstitious time and so it should come as no surprise that eight women of various ages believed the plate and followed

Haggleworth up the river to worship his penis. He landed on a bald, shale-covered scrap of earth not far from the river in northeastern Iowa. Because it could not be farmed Haggleworth was able to buy the property for a dollar and fifty cents. Three days into the new colony, tragedy struck. A great famine overtook the settlers, so the angel ordered Haggleworth to send some of his women to the river to worship other men's penises for money and food. It worked! Haggleworth was in business! A steady stream of boatmen beat a path to Haggleworth's church of penis worship over the next thirty years. Haggleworth lived to the ripe old age of forty-eight and died with a boner. That's what we were told anyway growing up in Haggleworth.

About ten years after Haggleworth's death, the Valley Coal and Iron Company bought the town for seventy-five cents and began mining for coal. Although the company changed hands many times over the next fifty years, Standard Oil of Iowa took over the operations in 1922 and successfully mined forty miles of intersecting tunnels of coal beneath the town. In 1940, the year I was born, Latham Nubbs flicked a half-chewed, still-lit stogie into the street outside of Kressler's Five and Dime and the town of Haggleworth caught on fire—a fire that still burns to this day. Deadly carbon monoxide gas and plumes of hell-spawned black smoke appear and disappear at random. The smell of sulfur, literally the smell of Satan himself, permeates the air, sending visitors and lost strangers to emergency rooms all over the state. In 1965 the governor of Iowa, Harold Hughes, condemned the town and relocated its remaining twenty-eight residents.

I was born into a simpler time. Environmental concerns wouldn't come into play until hippies and weirdos started crawling the earth. For us, growing up in Haggleworth, the fires were a way of life, a hazard like any other. The smell went unnoticed because it's what we knew. The black smoke rising from the hot earth was a daily reminder of the hell pit below the surface. I was born into this town of three hundred hardheaded Iowans whose only way of life was mining, and of course drinking and burning to death. Mining was especially hard because of the fire, and drinking wasn't any easier, also because of the fire. The more you drank alcohol, the more likely your chance of igniting yourself. It was a cruel irony, but the only way to stave off that horrible impending feeling of one day burning to death was to drink more . . . a vicious circle, really, but one we enjoyed with gusto.

In this carefree community the Burgundys were a proud clan. Claude and Brender Burgundy had eight boys. I was the last one born. The plain fact of the matter is we all hated each other equally. There were no alliances within the family. It was every man for himself. The day I was born was the day I received my first sock in the face. My brother Lonny Burgundy smacked me the first time he saw me. I couldn't speak yet, as I was only a few minutes old, but I do remember thinking to myself, "So that's the way it is." I grew to like the uncertain anticipation of being pounded on by my older siblings and by the occasional explosion of fire that jumped up out of the earth. In grade school, my best friend, Cassy Moinahan, and I were walking home when a sinkhole opened up and down he went into the fiery pit that was Haggleworth just below the surface. His screams of pain could be heard coming through the floor of the hardware store for two days. I came to recognize a kind of fluidity to life that has stayed with me from those early days. Every man takes a beating and every man gets dumped back into the earth . . . so why cry about it? Right?

My father, Claude Burgundy, was a learned man, educated in Oxford, England. He came to Haggleworth out of a deep respect for its unlivable conditions. His wife, and soul mate for life, Brender, was all class with tits out to here. I didn't much care for either of them but they were my parents and I loved them both dearly. On Saturday nights they went dancing over at the Elks Lodge. They never missed a Saturday night at the lodge. Just as soon as they were out the door it was every Burgundy for himself. Fists, chair legs, frying pans, railroad spikes—whatever was lying around the house we used to pummel the other guy. We all had our tricks. Horner set traps all over the house. Lonny carried a whip. Bartholemew welded himself a whole medieval suit of armor. Jessup had attack dogs. For me it quickly came down to Jack Johnson and Tom O'Leary, the names I gave my left and right fists respectively. With Johnson I was able to fend off most of the blows, but with O'Leary I could mete out my own share of pain. By the time I was ten years old even my oldest brother, Hargood, knew to keep away from O'Leary's leaden punishment. Johnson had them on their heels quick but O'Leary was the one that put them to sleep. Even to this day I've been known to call on O'Leary to clear up an argument or end some nonsense.

Years back I was in New York City and I found myself in a tricky situation with professional blowhard Norman Mailer. He and I had occasion to mix it up from time to time and I always had no problem stuffing his face back in his shirt. But he caught me off guard on this occasion. We were at Clyde Frazier's place on the Upper West Side of Manhattan. Mailer must have been waiting in a broom closet for me for more than an hour when he jumped out and began whacking at me with a hammer. I took as many blows as I could until I unleashed the Ole Doomsday from Dublin, Tom O'Leary. That was all she wrote for Norman. He probably took the nightmare of my knuckles to his grave. No sir, I've never been afraid to resort to fisticuffs. Not my first option, mind you. I've stepped on too many loose teeth to want anything to do with violence . . . but if it comes my way I know what to do.

It wasn't all fistfights and terror in Haggleworth. There were many days and nights of pure unabashed fun. For instance, for some unknown reason that really makes no sense at all, Haggleworth had the finest jazz supper club west of Chicago. It was called Pinky's Inferno. It made very little sense—it's almost unbelievable really—but there it was, a jazz club in a town of three hundred in the middle of nowhere. At age eleven I got a job as a busboy in Pinky's and a passion was born in me—a passion so strong I feel it to this day whenever I make love to a woman or see a sunrise or smell thick-cut Canadian bacon cooking, or whenever I report the news. It's a passion for jazz flute. It all started for me in 1951 at Pinky's Inferno. Diz, Bird, Miles—they all came through Haggleworth, unbelievable as that sounds, to play at Pinky's.

Even typing it now seems stupid. I was there at the time and I still want to fact-check this. I made my first flute out of a length of steel pipe my brother Winston tried to beat me with. Winston was my least-favorite brother, and that's saying a lot. He would beat you while you slept—clearly against the rules, but he didn't care. He was a union strike buster for many years before he was brained by a rock. Now he sells pencils in a little wooden stall in downtown Omaha. I buy twenty every Christmas. They say hatred and love are two sides of the same golden coin.

**THE END**

I loved that homemade pipe flute. Dizzy Gillespie used to make me get up onstage with him and play that thing until my mouth would bleed. Maybe I'm misremembering this part. I'll fact-check it one more time before I finally commit it to paper though. Dexter Gordon, Art Blakey, even the older guys, Louis Armstrong and Sidney Bechet, came by. Hey, I get it, if you don't want to believe any of this I can't blame you. Anyway, I picked up a little something from each one of these jazz masters—you know what? I think the whole "jazz flute" stuff should stay out of the novel, come to think of it. It's too ridiculous even if it did really happen. I will simply say this: Chet Baker and Gerry Mulligan taught me, an eleven-year-old boy, the rudiments of jazz improvisation in the alley behind Pinky's Inferno one night in Haggleworth, Iowa. That's solid enough information that is very believable. (I have no idea if this is going to hurt or help my credibility here, but just down the alley from us Jack Kerouac was getting a blow job from Allen Ginsberg. More than likely this can be corroborated in their own writings. Those guys wrote an awful lot.) With all these hep cats coming through Haggleworth in the fifties I became the source for their drug habits. I had an in with some of the dealers in the area and I would score smack for the musicians in exchange for music lessons. I quickly learned to cook it so they could fix up before their sets. Forget it. This sounds impossible to me. I know what happened but none of this reads real. I'm just going to go with this: I have a passion for jazz flute. I got it from somewhere. It's part of who I am. There.

When my brothers and I weren't beating on each other we would roam the streets looking for any other kind of fun we could get into. These days you would call us a "street gang" but in those days it was just considered horsing around. The regular folks of Haggleworth, when not scared of falling into the hot ground below their feet, were quite comically terrified of the Burgundys. There was a saying around Haggleworth that mothers told their children. It went something like this: "Eat your vegetables or the Burgundy boys will beat the living shit out of you." Silly really. Men would sometimes refer to a black eye as a "Burgundy." Derrick Burgundy, the second-oldest of my brothers, did do acts of violence that transcended the usual fun boy stuff and he was gunned down by a posse, which absolutely nobody had any objection to . . . but that was only

one Burgundy in eight who was a bad egg. Our reputation as
town bullies didn't mean much to us. We just laughed it all off
and had a good time. The only townsfolk who were not scared
of the Burgundys were the Haggleworths. They were the only
other prominent family in Haggleworth and because of their
last name they felt they owned the whole town. It was nonsense of course. Shell Oil owned Haggleworth. (That's why
there was no real government or police or any order whatsoever. It was the reason why my father, a strict Darwinist, loved
the town.) But the Haggleworths erected a museum in honor
of their founding father. Some of them still practiced their
pious religion of penis worship, but for the most part they
were an uncultured, rangy bunch of derelicts who ate cat food
and lived in caves. Some others lived on Willow Street in large
Victorian houses. They did manage to build one impressive
building downtown, a great big marble and granite Roman-
looking thing. It was a sort of clubhouse and harkened back
to a more forward-looking time in Haggleworth when money
was flowing into the city from foreign investors and sex per-
verts. They called this huge building "the Courthouse." They
even carved the name "Courthouse" into the stone above the
door. No one recognized it as an actual courthouse unless
you had to pay a ticket or get a marriage license. Shell Oil
certainly had no use for it. And no Burgundy ever stepped
foot in it as far as I know.

The Haggleworths really stuck their noses up at the rest of
us . . . which was laughable really, because they were descended
from whores mainly. A Burgundy, upon encountering a Haggleworth in the street, would make a point of reminding the

Haggleworth of his or her ignominious lineage with something pithy like "How's it going, son of a whore?" To which a Haggleworth might come back at a Burgundy with something like "When was the last time you took a bath?" (It was a fair blow as we never took them growing up.) Then a little boxing might ensue and depending on the number involved in the conflict some more pushing and shoving, and then usually a kind of riot would break out with fires and broken glass and such. Totally predictable small-town-type stuff. A bygone era really. Apple pie. Fishing villages. I had a lot of respect for the Haggleworth boys and girls. They could fight like devils. Many nights after a riot I would find myself limping home because they had gotten the best of me. I can laugh about it now. Heck, I laughed about it then.

And then there was Jenny Haggleworth. She was simply a dream. Every boy in town was in love with her. She was the kind of girl that if you saw her at the malt shop, your heart just stopped—fiery red hair, long legs, the softest hands, like two dove wings. Her eyes were like enchanted emeralds. She was a cross between Rita Hayworth and Grace Kelly, and me being twelve years old I was head over heels in love with her. She was twenty-eight and had a job in the mining office.

Because she was a Haggleworth and I was a Burgundy it was a forbidden love but one that I knew I would risk. I also knew that if ever my secret was revealed the whole Haggleworth clan would chase me down and throw me into Dutchman's Dungeon—a fire pit so deep and terrifying that years later when the Army Corps of Engineers were called in to cap it off they turned tail and ran out of there faster than baboons running from a ghost lion. To this day its location isn't on any map and is a well-kept government secret. I know how to get there, of course, as does anyone who grew up in Haggleworth, but we have all signed a presidential oath of secrecy demanding that we never reveal its whereabouts. Among many others over the years I took noted tennis legend and feminist Billie Jean King up there one night with the intent of throwing her in. I was steaming mad at her—I still am but I'm not a murderer. Billie Jean King knows the whereabouts of Dutchman's Dungeon; so do famed quarterback Roman Gabriel and legendary funnyman Dicky Smothers and many more. Jenny and I would meet in a small clearing in the woods that was unknown but to her and me. The sunlight splashed through the leafy canopy of maple and oak, dappling spots of light on a quiet glade no bigger than a bedroom. It was our hideaway. We talked and held hands, and occasionally I was rewarded with a kiss from her soft lips. I lived for those kisses. I saved our correspondences, which one day I will publish as *The Love Letters of Ron Burgundy and Jenny Haggleworth*. I think mankind would benefit greatly from reading them, with the disclaimer that these are the simple yearnings of a twelve-year-old boy addressing his love sixteen years his senior. Here are just a few exchanges.

*Dearest Jenny,*

*Each hour I spend away from you is another hour in torment. I cannot bear the distance our hearts must suffer! Purgatory knows no pain like the agony of our separation. My minutes are filled with anxious longing for a mere glimpse of your beauty. The ruby ringlets in your hair, like ribbons adorning a Christmas gift, await my unfurling! A poem I write to you! "So soft the cheek, so smooth the shoulders, the liquefaction of your clothes rippling over your huge boulders." Ron Burgundy, Haggleworth, Iowa, 1952.*

*I must see you. Until then, my heart beats only for your answer.*

*Your love servant, Ron Burgundy*

*Ron,*

*Got your letter. Meet in make-out woods after work.*

*Jenny*

*PS: Bring gum*

*Sweet Jenny,*

*I am beside myself with joy! Your encouraging words of our anticipated reunion and our innocent pleasures have placed me in a transcendent mood! God surely works a spirit through every living being and only love can open the window to its ebb and flow. I shall wait upon the hour in joyous anticipation. Your thoughts of shared love shall remain forever locked in my bosom awaiting a key that only you possess. Oh, Jenny Haggleworth! How the name itself floats and flutters like a butterfly over the fields of flowers. Our reunion cannot come fast enough. Not even Mercury himself with winged foot could bring about*

*our conjoining with the speed my heart so desires. I am forever*
*at your mercy and your undying worshipper, Ron Burgundy.*

*Ron,*

*Might be late. Gotta get some oil for my car. See ya.*

  *Jenny*

*PS: Bring gum*


Pages and pages of suchlike correspondence poured forth
from the two of us. Volumes of letters, enough to fill at least
forty leather-bound books. Some years back I saw an adver-
tisement in the popular fashion magazine *Jiggle* for a book-
binding device. It came with leather sheets, needles, high-test
threading and plans for a build-your-own press. I don't know
what I was thinking! I'm all thumbs when it comes to crafts!
Many of you may recall I did the news with my hands ban-
daged for a three-month stint. I explained on air that I had
rescued a child from a hospital fire. We found a baby and a
mother who needed a couple of bucks and set up a story, all
in good fun. What really happened was that I tried to bind
those letters with that complicated binding setup! I tore up
my hands pretty good. I got a chuckle out of that.

Eventually the lovers were discovered. In a town of three
hundred it's hard to keep a secret. The Haggleworth clan
found out I was diddling their sister and I was jumped and
roped and dragged behind Jenny's car as she drove through
the streets of Haggleworth. These were lawless days when

men took it upon themselves to impose justice. Jazz great Er-
roll Garner was in town doing a two-week stint at Pinky's Inferno. He saw me being dragged through town and went off
to get my brothers. I guess their hatred for the Haggleworths
was greater than their hated for me, because pretty quickly
all eight of the Burgundy boys were in town. A verbal back-
and-forth rapidly escalated to a situation where the National
Guard was called in. Some people were burned pretty badly,
that I do remember.

After the bloodiest day in Haggleworth history, Jenny and
I agreed it was best to take some time off. She left town one
night with jazz great Thelonious Monk and then was married
to Jack Paar for a while. I can't say for sure why Jenny Haggleworth, a twenty-eight-year-old model and Miss Iowa, was
so infatuated with a twelve-year-old boy, but I had a couple
of theories. One was pretty basic. At twelve I was already beginning to show signs of the future girth for which I would
become somewhat legendary. I could see, looking down into
my pants, something I would enjoy looking at and talking to
for many years to come. Some women have called it Pegasus,
after the winged horse of Greek mythology. The Lord Jesus
Christ works in mysterious ways when he hands out lower
body parts! Some men are blessed with extraordinary length
but not much girth. Others have been awarded great girth
but less length, and then . . . there are a select few who are
granted the whole wonderful package, girth and length. I'm
one of those guys who got just the girth. I wouldn't trade it
for nothing—except more length. I know for a fact Jenny
was transfixed by my reproductive parts because in some of

our more tender and romantic moments she would yell out, "Show me that stack of pancakes!" or "Gimme that can of beans!" My understuff was and has been a source of great pride for me but not my greatest. If I had to guess at what body part Jenny Haggleworth and a million other women were attracted to most I would have to say it was my hair.

# MY HAIR

First of all I'd like to dispel the nine most popular myths about my hair.

**MYTH NUMBER 1:** My hair is called Andros Papanakas. It is not. I have no name for my hair.

**MYTH NUMBER 2:** My hair was bestowed upon me by the gods. This one is hard to dispel. It would have been just like Zeus to make such a gift, or Hermes, but even though I have called on these two gods many times I have never been told specifically by either one that I was given my hair, so I have to say no to the gift-from-the-gods theory.

**MYTH NUMBER 3:** My hair is insured by Lloyd's of London

for one thousand dollars. Nope! It's fifteen hundred, thank you.

**MYTH NUMBER 4:** My hair won't talk to my mustache. This is basically true but I would hardly call that a myth.

**MYTH NUMBER 5:** My hair starred in the movie *Logan's Run*. It was definitely up for the part of Logan but that eventually went to Michael York. He did an excellent job in the film and to this day it's still considered the best film of all time.

**MYTH NUMBER 6:** My hair on my head is the exact same as the hair on my crotch. Don't I wish!

**MYTH NUMBER 7:** My hair was the principal cause of the overthrow of the Chilean government in '73. This one is true. Look it up.

**MYTH NUMBER 8:** Each strand of my hair carries the DNA for not only a complete Ron Burgundy clone but also a duck-billed platypus. This is incorrect. Scientists at Georgetown University studying my hair strands have detected the DNA from eight different semiaquatic mammals. The platypus is nowhere in sight.

**MYTH NUMBER 9:** I wear a toupee. Sure, I wear a toupee, and women don't have vaginas and cats don't have dongs! Seriously, this is not a myth, just an insult. Stop it. This is my hair. You can't have it. You can't buy it. You can't burgle it, but you can enjoy it on top of my leathery oversized head.

I would love to be able to report to you that my hair is

the work of many hours of teasing, combing, conditioning, dyeing, fluffing and whatever else men do for vanity's sake, but it's simply not the case. I was born with my hair and that's that. I could be cruising down the road in a new convertible sports car with a topless beauty queen at my side. She could be feeding me a thick New York strip steak and pouring me a tall glass of scotch as I drive. In the backseat of the car there could be a stuffed bear and Johnny Carson, but as that car sped by, most guys on the street would look up and say to themselves, "Man, I wish I had that hair." It's just a simple fact. My hair is great. I've always had it, literally, from the day I came out of the womb. From what I was told, on first seeing me come into this world the doctor and the nurse stood dumbfounded and then ordered the entire hospital into the delivery room because they thought perhaps they had witnessed the second coming of Christ! NO, they hadn't! It was just me, Ron Burgundy, and my perfect hair.

Ed Harken, my boss at Channel 4, once joked that if anyone ever cut my hair, like Samson I would lose my power. I laughed deeply and heartily for many hours and lost no sleep at all over his wit. Several days later, a little more anxious, I went to the San Diego Public Library and asked if they had any books on this Samson guy. Little-known fact, turns out he's mentioned in the Bible. It's just a blurb really but that's pretty cool to get a mention in the Bible! It wasn't a well-written story but I got the gist. It was comforting to know the whole story and I was able to function without much incident having this new knowledge of what happened to Samson's hair. Knowing all about Samson and his girlfriend Delilah did not make me nervous and I hardly spent any time thinking about what would happen if someone cut my hair off. It was fairly easy to not think about it, although at night for a few hours I would give it a thought. Why did he tell her? It made no sense! I guess women always want to know the source of our power. That's why they sleep with us, right, guys?

Anyway, I know that it calmed me immeasurably to know all about Samson and what happened to him. That's why I was surprised a few weeks later during our production meeting when I yelled out very loud, "Ed Harken, if you touch my hair I will cut your face up like a root grinder and your friends will spend the rest of their lives too terrified to look at the mess I left behind. Do you understand me! DO YOU!" I believe I had a twelve-inch hunting knife in my hand at the time I said it. Long story short: My hair is not mythological or magical in any way. It's very simply a great gathering of hair strands formed in such a way as to be undeniably perfect, and I am not nervous at all about someone cutting it off someday. That doesn't make me nervous.

Now, I know in the past you've seen pictures of me in the ad section of the *San Diego Union-Tribune* endorsing this or that hair product but I'm here to tell you it's all a lot of horse crap. I say and do a lot of stuff for money. One thing I've always stayed true to even if it meant never compromising is that Ron Burgundy is for sale. I'll endorse anything if there's money on the table. Seriously, if some dirty grease bag flies into town with a bottle of cat urine and pays me enough money to say it will make your hair look like mine, I'll do it. Just know your hair will never look like mine. That's not to say I don't on occasion use product. All anchormen use product. Most of the better hair products have either lost traction with today's youth or been discontinued by the EPA. Over the years these were the products I came to trust but that now no longer exist for one reason or another.

### FRED MACMURRAY'S MAN GUM

One of the best ever. Was the "go-to" hair product growing up. It came in a one-gallon bucket and had the consistency of axle grease. You could use it as axle grease in a pinch but at a quarter a gallon, why waste it? In the sixties they discovered that lead chips were not safe and Man Gum lost favor with hair lovers.

### HARMON KILLERBREW'S HEAD GOO

If you were a sports nut like me you couldn't wait to squeeze out a tube of Killerbrew's Head Goo before heading out to the movies. More like plaster of Paris than a malleable gel, it went on wet and minutes later you had a rock of hair on your head that no force could change for days. We just loved it. Like all plaster-based products in those days, the lime content was pretty high. One day it disappeared from the shelves with an offer to join in a class-action lawsuit. No harm no foul, I've always said. Baseball legend Harmon Killerbrew took the *r* out of his name and became "Killebrew." It was enough of a name change to hide him from the lawsuit and any culpability relating to all the seizures.

## EXXON HAIR TAR

This stuff was everywhere and it really did the trick. It was the only hair product with the words *Completely Edible* on the label. Not that you would eat it, because it tasted like farts and clams, but it got thrown into a lot of pastry recipes around where I grew up and no one cared a lick. It took a while to work it into your hair as it was pretty sticky stuff, but once it was applied, look out, James Dean. It also helped if you had black hair because that's the only color it came in. A shipment of Exxon Hair Tar spilled out on Route 66 in Indiana in '56 and they closed down the highway for half a year. Every animal and piece of vegetation was annihilated within ten miles of the spill. Sad, when you think about it. In a gesture of true American courage Exxon owned up to their goof by saying they were sorry for what the truck driver did and that truck driver would have been fired if he had lived. Gosh darn it! Sometimes I wish we all could stand so tall in the face of our failure!

## DR. LON'S LOVE SAUCE

Frankly this was the best of the bunch. It could only be found in adult bookstores and the backs of gentlemen's magazines, but if you got your hands on a tub of this creamy sauce it made all the rest look like turds. No one knew anything about Dr. Lon except that he was a real doctor who specialized in hairology and that he had discovered his sauce while hiking in Tibet. It smelled a bunch like socks and yeast, so you had to keep your distance from other people, but the glow it gave your hair was worth it. I liberally put this on my head three times a day for four years but then decided I needed human touch and I put it away. Years later I did a story on Dr. Lon, only to discover he was not a real human at all but just a made-up name. The real Dr. Lon was a bunch of researchers at Exxon Oil! Ingenious!

In the end, because I'm such a hobby lover, I concocted my own special hair formula through trial and error. It took six years to get the perfect balance but here it is, my gift to those of you who honor your hair with love and affection.

Eggs (six to eight)
Bourbon (half bottle)
Beer (Schaefer, four cans)
Maple syrup (bottle)
Rotten apples (four)
Coconut milk (one gallon)
Paint thinner (two cups)
Shoe polish (two tins)
Bouillon cubes (twenty)
Cat urine (bowl)
Wet newspaper (two to six pages)
Cream of broccoli soup (one can)

To prepare, throw all the ingredients into a large lobster pot and stir vigorously; add paint, color optional, when necessary. Cook till boiling and then let cool. Recipe makes enough for one or two applications. Your hair will look shimmery and stout all day. Hey . . . I'm just pulling your chain. My hair looks this way when I wake up and stays the same all day long. It's just something you're going to have to come to terms with. Unless your last name is Hudson, as in Rock, or Goulet, as in Robert, you won't even come close to hair like mine in your lifetime no matter what you plop on your head. Ron Burgundy.

One other quick story about my hair. In 1971 I was awarded the prestigious *Action-Man Magazine* award for best hair. It's quite an honor. Past winners have been Lorne Greene, Bobby Sherman, and professional golfer Johnny Miller, among others. So yes, it's a very big deal. The big shots over at *Action-Man Magazine* and Brunswick Bowling Balls fly the winners first-class to Hawaii for an all-expenses-paid weekend of fun and sun at Eros Hotel and Spa. Beautiful mixed-race nude women parade around with colorful drinks, sashaying between ice sculptures of scenes from the *Kama Sutra* and live exotic animals on chains. It's a first-class operation all around. Although I'm not the biggest celebrity at the gathering (Buddy Hackett and Agnes Moorehead are both in attendance!), I feel pretty at home surrounded by all this class and style. I plant myself at the Outrigger Bar and enjoy a whole menu full of ice-cream drinks while feasting on shrimp and hot dogs. I will admit straight up I'm doing my very best to put out some Burgundy sex signals. From the hotel gift shop I've purchased a bold new swimsuit and robe that are most definitely working. I am getting more than my share of looks! (That swimsuit was hands-down my favorite for years until my associate Brian Fantana told me it was a pair of women's underwear. Carpe diem!) Sure enough I lock eyes with a sultry temptress with a name tag that reads "Kimberly Gropff, Brunswick Bowling."

(For her protection—she is a married woman with children from Sterling, Illinois—I will call her "Tanya Lambkin." We later had relations in many different positions and styles, but that's not where this story is going, although it's hard not to think about it.) As "Tanya Lambkin" is making her way over to me at the bar and Sir Roderick Hainsworth is peeking out of my swimsuit (women's underwear), a sudden burst of crashing plates and general commotion explodes out by the pool. From where I'm perched I can barely make it out but someone is sing-yelling my name: "Rooooooon Buuuuuuurgundy! Yooooou are an imposterrrrr!" I think I've made it very clear I abhor violence of any kind but when it comes looking for me I sleuth out my chances and decide if I need to run away or stand my ground. "Rooooooon Buuuuuuurgundy! I knoooooow you're at this hooooooooteeeeel!" Almost more singing than yelling really. I stand, still uncertain if I'm going to take off or get ready for some boisterous action, but I've run out of time. Moving at me like a charging rhino is Hollywood legend and world-class singer Jim Nabors. I quickly sidestep his attack and give him a karate chop to the back of his head. Unfazed, he turns on me and swipes a bear-paw-sized fist at my head, which I fend off with my left (Jack Johnson, as you may recall). No time to lose! I bring Tom O'Leary from down below and come up strong on Nabors's chin. The big man hardly rocks back at all! Too much man there. I lay into him with some rabbit punches to his bread basket—nothing. Something like Thor's mighty hammer comes down on my head and I start to wobble. Jim Nabors, television's Gomer Pyle, is about to take me down. Time to get tricky. Like a boxer just trying to make it through a round, I dive at the big fella and grab on for dear life. I need to catch my breath—we dance like this for a few minutes. It starts to dawn on me that Nabors is enjoying the close contact with another man. He relaxes for a second and pow! Tom O'Leary right to the nut sack. Down goes Gomer in a Pyle! (Just too hard to resist. It's a chuckle for sure.) Once he's down I get into his mug. "Hey, what's the big idea?" He gives me a confused look for a second and then sheepishly admits, "Ahhh, someone said your hair was better'n mine and I got sore." Then he smiles and starts laughing. It's an infectious laughter so I start giggling too. Pretty soon we both are chuckling up a storm. We became friends. "Tanya Lambkin" invited the two of us up to her room along with Hawaiian lounge singer Don Ho. A lot of beef got passed around that night, if you know what I mean. Anyway, I thought I'd share that story about my hair.

# OUR LADY QUEEN
# OF CHEWBACCA

If the town of Haggleworth, with its burning streets and
ash heaps and high murder rate, was a grim place to grow
up, no effort was made inside the walls of Our Lady Queen
of Chewbacca High School to make us think otherwise. The
hallways of the high school were some of the most dangerous thoroughfares in town. Grown men didn't like walking
those halls. Because of the town's mining tradition, much of
the school was dug underground. If you weren't careful, one
wrong turn and you could get lost for days. Rumor had it that
somewhere in the deep, past the teachers' lounge and further
down into the subbasement, there was a Minotaur. It seems

almost too mythological to believe but this Minotaur, which did in fact exist, came from the deepest recesses in the earth. Minotaurs are born of fire and anger. No man can kill one unless equipped with the arrow of Theseus. Ahhh, now I'm just listing Minotaur facts to show off! You got me! Anyway, there probably was a Minotaur in the basement of my high school but it's one of those unconfirmed facts. There were, however, some classrooms that kept a canary in a cage in the corner. The oxygen could get pretty thin on some days, and if that canary dropped it was an unorganized scramble to see who could get out alive.

Carrying my flute through the halls with my impossibly beautiful hair put a fat bull's-eye on my back from the beginning. I knew if I was going to make it through those four years I needed to find the toughest guy in school and show him I was not one to be trifled with. On my first day I went right up to Han Solonski, a big lump of a Pole, and I beat him within an inch of his life. The poor dumb lug didn't know what hit him. (It was a brick. I used a brick.) After that day no one dared bother me. I was number one. No one ever officially declared that I was number one, but I knew it. I had posters made. It was pretty obvious.

I can't say I was much of a student. The good sisters, bless their hearts, showed a lot of patience with me but it just didn't take. A word about the good sisters, and all nuns for that matter. I'm no Catholic; in fact I have an irrational and unexplainable dislike for the Catholics. They're a grubby bunch of sour sacks if you ask me, but even the Catholics I talk to hate nuns. I mean, you're always hearing about stone-faced old hags rapping kids on the knuckles for not paying attention or stern old maids pulling children through the halls by their ears. First of all, if any nun would have tried any kind of nonsense like that in Haggleworth they would have gotten socked in the puss. I would have been the first in line to do the socking. I've socked old ladies before and believe me, it's not pretty. But the nuns at Chewbacca who tried to put education in me were nothing like the repressed old maids we all think of when we think of nuns. No, I don't know why—maybe it was a papal order from the Vatican—but the nuns we got at Our Lady Queen of Chewbacca were very sweet and very, very gorgeous. The whole lot of them across the board could have been *Playboy* centerfolds for sure, but they gave their lives over to Jesus Christ. There were about twenty-five of them there in the high school and they ranged from age eighteen to twenty-two. Jesus was their lord and master, and what a lucky guy he was, because these ladies were absolutely stunning. Maybe God sent the very best to Haggleworth because it was so close to hell. Who knows? All of them were five foot seven inches tall and built like Raquel Welch, with legs that went on for days.

Of course, we never saw the nuns out of their habits and hats, except when they taught wrestling or during swim class, but other than those two hours every day they were as buttoned up as Eskimos in a snowstorm. I'm gonna admit it: When one of those nuns showered with us after wrestling practice there were more than a few boners on display. It wasn't very respectful of us but it was hard not to think of them as just ordinary women even though they had given over their lives to serve only Jesus Christ. Heck, we were all just boys with very little understanding of religious conviction. Lando Calrissian, the only African American (still getting used to saying it like that!), made a play for Sister Honeytits (I'm not making that name up. Why would I make that name up?) but that was the only instance I knew of such fiddling about. Lando was the star shooting guard for the Chewbacca Stormtroopers, so he was basically immune to punishment anyway. One of the sisters, Sister Vicky Vaginalicious (real name), did leave the faith and took up with my good buddy Wedge Antilles, but it was rare. These women respected the church too much to let carnal desire interfere with their calling.

Every year as part of a charity drive for the local hospital the nuns would do a fun pageant for the students and the parents. The students would make animal costumes and put on a show with singing and some kind of story. Most of the time I was a friendly raccoon or a squirrel and I showed off my flute playing. It was really a great night for the proud parents. Then the auditorium would start to fill up with mine workers and out-of-towners and we children would be asked to leave. The rest of the show was performed by the nuns, who would, for charitable reasons, strip off their habits for the night and, because they had sacrificed their lives to Christ, put on six-inch heels and colorful lingerie and do up their hair and look like real Italian movie stars! Most of them could have been Italian movie stars! Not one of them was less beautiful than Sophia Loren in her prime. Imagine twenty-five basically naked young women in lingerie and heels walking back and forth onstage in a wonderful show of faith and charity and religious servitude. If they weren't nuns you would have thought they were strippers! But of course they were nuns and no one could see them as anything else. For my own part, it was almost enough to make me a convert if my hatred of the Catholics had not been so irrational and visceral. Between the two shows we would sometimes get twenty to forty thousand dollars for the night in donations. The principal, Monsignor Morty Grossman, would sometimes have the sisters do the same "act," as he called it, up in Chicago, where they would make even more money! The kids were never invited to Chicago or Memphis or Kansas City but the monsignor would always tell us it was a huge success when he would roll back into town in his limo. I may not look back on Haggleworth with much fondness but whenever I see a nun, despite my almost limitless and completely unfounded hatred for Catholics, I do remember those sweet, innocent and, I'll say it, ridiculously sexy nuns at Our Lady Queen of Chewbacca.

Here's something you might not have known about me: I was a joiner in high school. Flag Folders Club, Glee Club, Drama Society, Taxidermy Society, Friends of Jazz, Society of Mineral and Rock Collectors, Jolly Jesters, United Socialist Party, Freudian Study Group—I did just about everything. I went out for all sports and I loved them all, but basketball was to me what horses are to twelve-year-old girls—some weird transferred sexual energy that really is more physically fulfilling than actual sex. Which is to say I just loved basketball. I did! I wasn't too good at it though. I was a brawler more than a player. "Five Fouls Burgundy" is what they called me. I got put into games for one reason and one reason only—to foul and to foul hard. I wanted guys on the opposing team to look across half court and worry about whether I was coming in the game. Sometimes opposing teams did their best to eliminate me way before game time, because if they didn't they knew I was going to come in and start throwing elbows. A team from the Quad Cities once tried to run me over in a parking lot a week before game time. If teammate Darth Blortsky wasn't there to push me out of the way I wouldn't be here today. Believe me, they ended up paying for their little prank on the court with some hard, hard, completely legal fouls. I got thrown out of the game that night! I was thrown out of every game, but not before I got my five in. I still hold the Iowa state record for most technicals in a season. Look it up.

We had a great team in '57: a big Swede named Swen Vader at center; a nimble power forward named Luke Walker; Brad Darklighter was our small forward; a lightning-fast little Italian, Vinny Cithreepio, ran the point; and Lando Calrissian shot the lights out as our number two. Obiwan Kanobi, an exchange student from Japan, was always good for six points as well. We won state that year but were later disqualified, as a lot of those guys had played semi-pro ball in Brazil; some of them were in their thirties. Nowadays people check that kind of stuff out, but back then we had a lot of thirty- and forty-year-old men posing as high school students. It was just something you did.

## QUICK SIDE NOTE

Okay, here's something completely unrelated to this book but I'm not writing another word till I get this off my chest. It's literally paralyzed me. I can't work. I can't sleep. I can't do anything. My neighbor Richard Wellspar came over here last Wednesday and borrowed my leaf blower. It's a Craftsman, so you can't go wrong there. Anyway, I'm a good guy so I let him borrow it. I go back in the house and start writing again. I don't even think about it for two or three hours, but then I see Richard out in his driveway and yell over to him, "Did you get a chance to use that leaf blower?" To which he says, "No." If that's not weird enough, it gets weirder. He then proceeds to talk about his new clients instead of keeping the leaf blower conversation going. He's some kind of high-end pool sales-man and he's always talking about his customers as "clients." Okay, so I go back in the house but I'm kinda miffed. I'm thinking, "When is he going to use the frickin' leaf blower so I can get it back?" Sure enough, the whole day goes by and I don't hear the leaf blower—then the next day, same thing. Well, now I can't work. I'm just sitting in my living room in silence waiting to hear the leaf blower. The anticipation is unbearable. Why did he ask to borrow it if he's not going to use it? Several days go by and now here we are! He hasn't even used it. He borrowed it and never used it! It's not about the stupid leaf blower. I could go buy ten of them tomorrow! I'm doing very well thank you. I'm the kind of guy who will walk into a Sears and buy three suits, a vacuum cleaner and four new tires and think nothing of it! It's about integrity! Being a good neighbor. The social contract. Anyway, I simply had to get that off my chest and now back to the writing! Not another thought about it.

# A FAMILY
# OF ANCHORMEN

My father, Claude Burgundy, was a natural-born News Anchor, as was his father and his father before him. Of course there was no television or radio station in Haggleworth, Iowa. Instead, every Friday night he would set up a desk in the Tight Manhole, an Irish bar where the mine workers drank and sang songs of misery. The oil company paid him to report on all the charitable and civic-minded projects they had in the works as well as hard-hitting news stories happening in Haggleworth. Because of his honest face and gifted speaking voice, men and women would come in from all the other bars in Haggleworth—the Dirty Chute, the Mine Shaft, the Rear

End, the Suspect Opening, the Black Orifice, the Poop Chute, too many to list here—all to listen to *The Shell Oil Burgundy Hour*. In Haggleworth it was the most popular show on Fridays at ten P.M. for years. It consistently beat out *Dragnet* and Ernie Kovacs in the local ratings. He would report high school sports scores, weddings, divorces, births, who was diddling who, but mostly good news about the oil company and their interests. I would come and watch from the front row and be transfixed by his smooth delivery and sharp tailoring.

One day, the fire that continued to burn under Haggleworth leaped over into tunnel 8, the most profitable tunnel in the whole coal operation. Unlike the fire that occasionally shot up from the earth and burned cars or dogs, this fire was getting in the way of profit and had to be contained. Men were sent down into the shaft to try and stop the fire, but it was no use. Eleven men died. The whole town was in a somber mood when my father got up to deliver the news. "Good evening, I'm Claude Burgundy and this is how I see it." (That's how he started every *Burgundy Hour*.) The bar was quieter than usual as they hung on every word. "Today, the Shell Oil Company of Iowa announced a new plan to bring multicolored blinking lights to downtown Haggleworth for the upcoming holiday season." On a day when eleven miners had burned to death, and husbands and fathers of people sitting in that bar had died, the Christmas-light story was the lead. A woman in the back shouted something at my father. Another man called him a coward. He just sat there, taking insult after insult as he bravely continued on with a story about a precocious little dog that wore a hat around town that everyone loved. He reported a story about a planned two-hole golf course. There was an in-depth interview with a woman who had won second place at the state fair for her lemon bars. It was great news and slowly people began to smile. When he got to his sign-off ("And that's what happened this week in Haggleworth") they were sad to see him go and could hardly wait for the next week's news.

In a candid moment as we were walking home that night I asked my old man why he didn't talk about the eleven men who had died or the culpability of the oil company or the environmental impact of this new deadly fire or the emotional damage many deaths could have on a small community like ours or even the plain fact that without tunnel 8 most of the town would be out of work. "Ron, sometimes people don't want the truth. They just want the news." I'll never forget these sage words from my father. Up until that point I made no distinction between "truth" and "news." I had thought they were one and the same! I was a boy of course and the world was just a kaleidoscope of butterscotch candies and rum cookies. I didn't understand the reason for news until that day.

I knew from a very early age that I would be a News Anchorman. I had great hair, for one, which is 70 percent of the job. I also had the pipes. I was blessed with my father's golden tones and melodious speaking voice. By the time I left Our Lady Queen of Chewbacca High I could read a document out loud from forty feet away without ever stumbling over a word. A photograph from shortly after my graduation shows me looking much the same way I do now. In fact at age eighteen I looked exactly as I do today. Women found me irresistible.

They still do find me irresistible. It's worth mentioning but not so important to the narrative at this moment. I mention stuff like that not for vanity's sake but because it simply needs to be said.

It was all lining up perfectly. Every year the National News Association of Anchormen, NNAA, sends out over a thousand representatives to find fresh new anchorman talent across the land. Prospects are invited to a brutal six-day camp to test their mettle through grueling challenges and photo shoots. It's a make-or-break week for young anchormen. An anchorman scout traveling through Haggleworth noticed me in the eighth grade but was not allowed to talk to me until I graduated. (After it was discovered that Edward R. Murrow was paid illegally by CBS as a four-year-old without his parents' consent, new guidelines were put into place to protect children from getting money.) By the time I graduated several scouts were interested in me. I was invited to Williamsport, Pennsylvania, to the anchorman camp—the "Gauntlet," as it's known in news circles. The field that year was tough—my class alone had News Hall of Famers Peter Jennings, Ted Koppel and Jim Lehrer. Vance Bucksnot, who became the number one anchor for the Quad Cities, was there, as was Punch Wilcox, the legendary anchor for Salt Lake City's KPAL. There was also Snack Reynolds (Austin), Brunt Harrisly (Columbus), Tink Stewart (Butte), Race Bannon (Minneapolis), Hit Johnson (Albany), Kick Fronby (Charlotte), Ass Perkins (Mobile) and Lunk Brickman (Boston). All of these men distinguished themselves with long careers for their respective stations, so yeah, it was very competitive.

The main goal of the Gauntlet was to test if you had the avocados for anchorman work. Could you hold your liquor? Could you tell the difference between bespoke and off-the-rack suits? Could you seduce women through a camera lens? Test after test of skills. Could you turn your head sideways to other news team members when speaking? Could you manufacture a laugh after reading a lighthearted story? Could you muster a knowing, disapproving head shake after a story of sadness? On and on for two, sometimes two and a half hours a day! If it were not for the fun diversions to be had in Williamsport I would have gone crazy! But fortunately Williamsport, Pennsylvania, is one of the wildest places I know. The key parties alone—and this is way before they had caught on around the rest of the country—were almost too decadent. I'm just going to assume that most people who live in Williamsport, Pennsylvania, to this day moved there to engage in terrifyingly adventurous sexual activity. I mean, how else could you account for the reckless bacchanalia that happened in that town every night? As a small-town boy in a big city for the first time I was warned of some of the dangers, but no one prepared me for what went on in that town. Maybe it's because it's not on the main east-west highway, Interstate 80, or maybe because the town is sufficiently surrounded by vegetation, lending itself to an isolationist mentality. Whatever has caused the town to feel cut off from the rest of civilization has also ensured its disconnect from the laws of man. It is a town of pleasure-seeking animals only gratified by buttery foods and genital friction. It's a wonderful place to be for a week and provides great relief from stress, but if you lived there, as was borne out by the people I met, you were little more than a skin-wrapped blob of insatiable carnal urges. Many people in Williamsport, Pennsylvania, walk around town with their mouths open, their pants down and their dicks flopping around.

At the end of the week I had distinguished myself enough at the Gauntlet to receive six promising offers for News Anchor. I leapt at Tucson. In a real show of Burgundy independence I stole the family car and never looked back. Good-bye Haggleworth, Iowa, hello Tucson. The drive east was delicious. I drank up the scenery like a man freed from prison. Two straight days I drove until I overheard two truckers outside of Washington, DC, say that Tucson was in the West. I should have looked at a map but in those days they didn't have maps, so off I went to the West. I felt like a young Horatio Alger traveling west to make my fortune. A few days later I was in the middle of Florida and getting kind of frustrated. I sometimes wonder how long-haul truck drivers even do it. How do they get from one destination to the next without getting lost? The stars? Anyway, once I got straightened out of Florida I was on my way. I went through Alabama, then Mississippi, then Arkansas, then Missouri and back through Iowa, up through Minnesota into Canada and then back into North Dakota and South Dakota and over into Wyoming, down through Colorado and Utah and Nevada and up through Idaho and back into Wyoming and Montana and into Idaho and Washington, down through Oregon to California and over to Arizona and over to New Mexico, where I had one of those "hey, wait a minute" moments where I thought maybe I had gone right through Arizona, so I turned around. When I landed in Tucson I hadn't slept in three weeks, and I hadn't shaved or showered. My suit smelled like eggs and butt and was stiff from all the sweat and dirt I'd built up on the road. Big problem: I was due on the air in five minutes! It was my first time on camera . . . and I knocked it out of the park. The station got hundreds of calls claiming a caveman had just reported the news. I got a chuckle out of that one. I worked for that station for about half a year until I found out it was in Albuquerque and not Tucson, and then off I went again until, about a month later (it's like twenty thousand miles from Albuquerque to Tucson if you take the direct route through Maine), I finally arrived at my first real job as the nightly News Anchor for WKXM Tucson.

# BREAKING HORSES THE BURGUNDY WAY

I've owned many horses over the years. I've had racehorses, plow horses, trick horses—you name it, I've owned it. I once bought a whole herd of wild horses up in Wyoming from a man in a big cowboy hat. He had no right to them at all but I bought them. I guess you could say I was conned out of six hundred bucks in that case. You could definitely say that! Anyway, breaking a horse can be a challenging but rewarding experience. Through very long and patient study it's a skill that I have mastered through my ability to whisper to horses.

I start off by gently whispering in their ear, "My name is Ron Burgundy and I respect you, great and proud animal.

Your lineage from winged Pegasus on down to Trigger is well-known to all. I too am well-known. I am a very popular News Anchor and I do quite well with the ladies, if you know what I mean. What else . . . oh, here's something—you, sir, are a piece of shit and I own you. Did you hear me? I own you and you are basically my bitch. So you might as well stop dicking around, okay? I need you to stop dicking around, 'kay?" Remember, all this is whispered so gently in the horse's ear. I continue with "Know this: I represent one thing and one thing only to you, and that is death. You are living on this earth because I choose to let you live, so you better get your shit together fast or you will be dog food. Got it, friend? Good. Good horse." Horses respond in a myriad of ways but I find, like children, if you can break them down fast to a place where they are nervous and uncertain about everything, building them up is more fun. It doesn't always work but I would say I have about a 5 percent success rate.

For about a two-month period I rode a horse to work in San Diego. It was an ordeal. I would whisper stuff in that old gal's ear every day but she never quite got the point. Finally, the traffic and honking, the fast food and always being stuck inside my office took their toll. I ended up dumping her on my friend Mac Davis for a few bucks, and wouldn't you know it, that horse went on to win the Santa Anita Derby two years running and showed up in the movie *The Wild Bunch*! It was as if the horse had a new lease on life and made a conscious decision to enjoy each and every day. Horses, you just gotta love 'em!

# MY NEIGHBOR AGAIN . . .

The Richard Wellspar ordeal continues. You'll remember that he's the deranged neighbor who "borrowed" my Craftsman leaf blower. We made eye contact as he was entering his house this evening. I just happened to be sitting in one of my dining room chairs on my front lawn very casual-like so he wouldn't suspect anything. He gets to his door, checks his mailbox and then turns his head and looks right at me! I give him a little wave and he nods his head. Nothing! Nothing about the leaf blower! I would laugh if it wasn't so serious. This is becoming a tragedy on an epic scale. I sat motionless for about an hour and then went back inside.

Anyway, Baxter and I have decided it's time to ratchet up the stakes in this game of chicken. Tonight I'm going to take my garbage can and unload the contents—old food and junk mail mostly—into his pool. Wish me luck!

# THE BEST NEWS TEAM
# OF ALL TIME

When I got to San Diego there was nothing. The station was a washed-up losing affiliate sharing space with a bakery. Rats walked across the floor in the middle of the day for no other reason than being bored. The station had no original programming to speak of and the news team consisted of an old lady who read the newswire and then made up stories. It was known all around San Diego that Channel 4 lied about the news every night. The lead story was often a story about the racetrack, because that's where the news team spent most of their time. There was no sports desk and no field reporting. The anchor was a man by the name of Chalk Munson. He was not a handsome man, nor was he well-spoken, nor could he hold his liquor. He barely made it through a broadcast without the aid of a four-letter word. He was beloved by no one in San Diego. When Ed Harken broke the news to him that he was getting fired he collapsed on the floor and started bawling—he had been praying for the day but thought it would never come. Every night, being forced to read the news was torture for him. He just assumed he would be doing it until he died. He frequently dreamed that he would be hit by a bus. It was his only escape he thought. I never met Chalk Munson but I do know that a large population of News Anchors feel trapped by their own chosen line of work. It's a lot of pressure to deliver the news night after night and some guys can't take it. Current newsman Wolf Blitzer hates his job and you can tell it every time he opens his mouth. Talking on camera for him is like one giant exhale, like he's trying to empty all his oxygen out of his body so he can die and free himself of the terrible pressure. Chris Wallace would rather live in a hobo camp than deliver the news, but he's up there, taking his lumps like a man. You can tell Brian Williams hates his job, but what's he going to do? He'd make a great pharmacist in my opinion. He should go to pharmacy school and bone up on drugs and get a job at CVS or Duane Reade. Being a News Anchor is not a job for the faint of heart. I took the job at Channel 4 because I recognized a challenge. That's me! I'm driven to be the very best.

The first order of business was the news team. Every one of the big stations was getting news teams in the sixties, and I knew we needed a great one. Ed Harken informed me that he too had been thinking about a news team and he was already looking for the guys to help me. I stopped him right there and told him I didn't want anyone but me putting together my team. We fought. No lie; we fought hard. Suits were ruined and coffeepots were broken, but in the end I won the fight. Little did he know I had already found one member of the team.

As it so happened I met Champ Kind my first week in San Diego. I came in from Denver on the bus and found a flop-house across from the station with rooms to let for one dollar a week. This was the early sixties, mind you, and San Diego has cleaned up its act since those rough-and-tumble days, but back then it was no place for honest Americans. I spent my first night out on the fire escape trying to stay cool in the midnight air, playing my flute as police sirens and gunshots went off all over town. It was a lonely time for me. After that first night I spent my evenings in some of the dirtiest low-down bars in town. Bars with names like the Filthy Slug, the Rusty Axe, the Toothless Sailor. Tough guys and loose ladies drank themselves to death in places like these, and I felt right at home.

One night I was stumbling back to my cold-water flat when four thugs jumped me in an alley. It was a real boisterous scuffle. I got hit everywhere, in the head and neck and ribs, but I gave back as good as I got. I put three of them on the ground pretty quick but the fourth guy was a real tangler. We beat on each other for a good half hour, circling and striking like two spotted hyenas. When it started to look like there wasn't going to be a clear victor I yelled *uncle*. We both put our fists down and had a good hearty laugh. He introduced himself as Champ Kind. I could tell we were going to be fast friends right then and there. In a loveless town full of empty souls and desperate men, I had found my first buddy. We tore it up. Some of our bar fights are now part of San Diego legend. They are the only bar fights I know of that have been given names: "the Punch-'Em-Up of '66," "the Black-Eye Derby," "the San Diego Bone Bonanza" and many more. I will tell you this: Champ has no scruples whatsoever. He will kill a man, probably has, for no reason at all. Well, I asked Champ why he jumped me and he said he just likes to throw his fists around from time to time and get knocked about and punched, and then he yelled out, "Whammy!" and that was that. He said *whammy* way too much. Every time he finished a drink, "Whammy." Ordering a sandwich, "Whammy." He had sad whammies and happy whammies and sometimes he would throw a whammy into a sentence where it made absolutely no sense, like "This Texas barbecue whammy so delicious, whammy." It might have been Tourette's. A lot of doctors told me it was Tourette's. Whatever it was, it was pure gold on air. I asked him if he knew anything about sports and he said he didn't but that he knew how to read and get excited. Well, I brought him in to Ed Harken and we both agreed that the best sports announcers are the ones who know how to read and get excited. If you had a young Jewish kid or a Chinese kid or college kid good with statistics, they could write the copy, but you needed a big dumb American male to yell out the sports. Champ Kind was perfect. "Whammy" became a household word in San Diego. Several restaurants offered "the Whammy," which was nothing more than ham on white bread, but it sounded fun. The Padres had "Whammy Day" at the park, where the first five thousand got Champ Kind bobbleheads. Every year some poor soul was trampled but they still do it to this day. It's worth the trade-off. If you ever get a chance make sure to pick up a copy of Champ's self-penned autobiography, *Whammy!* It's not always the most fun read. There's more darkness than light for sure, but still, it lets you in on a fascinating life of ups and downs. I wouldn't read more than twenty pages at a clip. It can really darken your mood for the day. It's definitely too revealing but that's Champ.

The next step was finding a field reporter. I've known a few in my time. Geraldo Rivera comes to mind. He's probably the best there is behind Brian Fantana. Of course no one is smoother and more professional than Brian Fantana. In my opinion he is the very best. It takes a special man to hit the streets and investigate stories, interviewing people while also being on camera. It's no easy job and it demands a certain kind of sex appeal. Geraldo had it. Brian Fantana had it in spades! He hooked up with women every time he took a camera crew out of the building. His secret: Only go after the best! That's what his secret was. I sometimes questioned what he meant by "the best." I mean, he basically went after anything with tits. I think maybe he thought women, just women in general, all women, were "the best," but that translates on camera. You can see it in Geraldo too. You just know he's rolled around with some homely fatties for sure and I'll bet you he didn't love them any less for the fun. That was Fantana's approach as well. Women just liked him because he never judged.

Anyway, before we found Fantana, Champ Kind and I were inseparable. After work we hit the bars and then went home. We roomed up together in those early days to save on bills. A lot of nights we would invite some of the guys from around the station or over at the bus depot to watch some nudie flicks. Champ had boxes and boxes of eight-millimeter film strips with all kinds of romantic action going on. Well on one such occasion the whole lot of us were struck dumb by an actor in one of the films. It was a short ten-minute thing called *A Lonely Girl Calls Up for Room Service*. If you're over fifty you know how these films go. So when the room service guy comes into the room—even before the pants came off—we were all just staring at the most handsome man with the greatest face for film ever. We never even got to the sex part. There were about ten guys and one lesbian and a he-she in the room and we just kept going back to the point in the film strip where this handsome devil entered. We did it over and over again until it hit me: "This guy needs to be our new field reporter." Ed Harken was in the room and he says, "What if he's an idiot or can't read?" Champ wasn't convinced either: "Hold your horses, Ron, most of these films are made in Sweden. We can't hire a Swede!" Well, I was hooked. I didn't care what these guys said; I had to find this guy and make an offer even if it meant going to Sweden.

The box the film came in said JACK PEPPER PRODUCTIONS on it and with a little quick calling around I discovered a business by that name up in the San Fernando Valley area of Los

Angeles. Champ and I took the bus up there and several buses to North Hollywood out in the Valley. It was hotter than shit, that I do remember. Jack Pepper Productions was a house out on Saticoy Street. Nothing fancy, just a little stucco prefab deal. The kind you see all over Southern California if you're not careful. Jack himself was in the back, by his pool, shooting a movie. He didn't exactly welcome our intrusion but Champ and I can be pretty persuasive with our fists. Pretty quickly everyone making the movie took a ten-minute break while we talked to Mr. Pepper. We showed him the film. He confessed it was one of his but he had no idea where the actor was. His name at the time of shooting the movie was Cyrus Court. Pepper was quick to tell us that these guys changed their names faster than Esther Williams changed costumes in *Million Dollar Mermaid*. Well, that's what he said. It's not like I'm making any of this up. He went on to say, "Cyrus Court could be any number of guys out there, Tony Oakland, Wayne Duke, Kevin Dangle and a lot more. The plain truth is most of these guys end up on Hollywood Boulevard hustling for tricks." Well, it was a pretty sad picture really. Here we thought this guy, Cyrus Court, had it made being in the movie business and having sex and all but Jack Pepper painted a different picture. Pepper's world was one of broken homes, drug use and loose morals. We went back outside by the pool to watch some filming but sitting there in the 110-degree heat, watching two people have sex like that, took all the spirituality out of it for me. It was as close as I've ever come to understanding what existentialism means. I lost sight of whatever theological center there is that holds us together, however loosely, while watching two very beautiful people with perfect anatomies go at it like dogs. In his defense Champ Kind turned to me and said quite simply, "Let's go, Ron. This ain't love."

We gave up on finding the actor in the film. If Pepper was right the kid was probably one pill short of an overdose, if not already dead. Before heading back to San Diego we decided to take in some music along the Sunset Strip. It was the midsixties and the Strip was where it was happening. We must have looked like a couple of old fuddy-duddies at the Whisky a Go Go but we paid our five bucks to see Johnny Rivers and forget our troubles. I don't have much use for long-haired people and man, there were a lot of them in the Whisky that night. The band that opened for Johnny Rivers was called the Practical Figs. They came out dressed in eighteenth-century garb with some guitars and started making noise—a lot of noise, really too much noise. Champ got disoriented and started swinging his arms around hoping to hit someone. I started yelling and then singing and then yelling. It was a crazy mess! If that's rock and roll then no thanks! They were barely into their first "number" when I grabbed Champ and said, "There he is!" It was Cyrus Court or Tony Oakland or whoever he was—the guy from the film up onstage as the lead "singer" of this "band." Champ rushed the stage and tackled him right away. It was the wrong thing to do and we acknowledged that. We did a bad thing. The crowd of hippies and drug addicts pounced on us and called us "the fuzz" and "narcs" and "Dad"—hurtful stuff, really, since we were none of those things. I might have been a dad but I certainly didn't know it. Anyway when the melee was over and the cops had gone I got a chance to talk to Tony Oakland. Right out of the gate he told me his name was Lance Poole. It wasn't his real name but the name he'd had for the last two months fronting the Practical Figs. He did the porn thing and scraped up enough dough to get through UCLA as a journalism major. The whole rock thing was a goof—just good college-guy fun and a great way to score chicks. I had him! I told him about the gig down in San Diego, where he could not only use his journalism degree but he could score all the chicks he wanted. He was looking to get out of that scene anyway and he agreed to give it a try for a few weeks. A few weeks became thirty years in the news game—eight Peabody Awards, a Mr. San Diego Award, six daytime Emmys, and a *Playgirl* spread. His real name was Brian Fantanofskavitch, which sounded too commie for comfort, so we changed it to Fantana and the rest is history. Ratings at the station went up the very moment he came on camera. Women wrote in to the station to complain they were having spontaneous and uncontrolled orgasms when he spoke. It was a real problem. For about a three-year period from '72 to '75 the news van was nothing more than a traveling bedroom for Fantana. We did way too many breaking stories from the suburbs. Real news might have been happening downtown or over at the harbor but Fantana liked trolling the suburbs for bored housewives. I would lead in with a line like "And Brian Fantana with a special report on crime in the suburbs" or maybe "Backyard barbecues, are they safe? Brian Fantana weighs in!" I mean, there were nights when I would throw to him with nothing and he'd make up a story standing outside a house he'd just come from. "Ron, I'm standing here on the corner of Mountain View and Grove, the virtual epicenter of a frightening new trend in exercising called 'jogging.'" Back at the station we had a hard time keeping a straight face. We knew what Fantana was up to. We supported it. It was good for ratings and frankly speaking it was good news. Veronica Corningstone, my wife and massage partner, ruined all that fun male stuff for us—in a good way of course.

The last member of the news team was our weatherman. We knew to really put us over the top we needed a great weatherman. It wasn't going to be easy. A team is about chemistry and a bad weatherman can ruin the mix. I've seen it happen before. A weatherman named Len Front was added to the number one Channel 2 news team in Denver back in '68. The team had been number one for at least ten years. Their longtime weatherman, Jerk Watson, was hit by lightning, which burned a red and blue mark across his face, making him virtually impossible to look at. I'm not going to hide my feelings when I say I never could forgive David Bowie for stealing the only thing Jerk had left, his red and blue streak, for his *Aladdin Sane* record. People would see poor Jerk Watson on the street where he sold wind-up toys and tease him about the terrible David Bowie impression. Jerk Watson was the first person with a red and blue streak through his face and he never saw a dime for it. Anyway, Len Front replaced him; the chemistry was wrong and the station dropped in the ratings faster than the Octomom drops babies. (NOTE TO SELF: Is there a better line for that? Probably not but give it some thought. Maybe put a clock on it. If you can't get a better line in three hours, then just leave it. It's really extremely funny but maybe a little too hip.) It wasn't Len Front's fault that the ratings dropped. He went on to become one of the great weathermen of all time over in Laramie but the chemistry was off in Denver and it tanked the whole operation. I don't think the importance can be overstated: If a news team makes a mistake in its weatherman they might as well change their names and leave the country or face the consequences of a life of shame.

We canvassed the country for just the right guy. He had to know meteorology. He had to be nice—a little too nice and too happy. He had to be clean. Most important, he had to come across like a simpleton or a village idiot. A lot of guys came into the station, mostly overweight guys who had clowning skills and useless meteorology degrees from tech institutes and third-tier colleges. Guys with names like "Hap" and "Doc" and "Cappy" came through the door but none of them had the mettle for the kind of team I was putting together. I think we looked at well over a thousand laughing idiots. We were just about to give up when it hit me—we needed to be active in the search. Where do weather guys come from? How can you spot one? We all got in a room and came up with a scientific list of what to look for.

## THE PERFECT WEATHERMAN

Must be nice.
Should carry lunch in a kid's lunch box.
Should live with mother.
Remembers the birthday of everyone he's met.

Listens to transistor radio at bus stop.

Likes watching softball games in park.

Enjoys petting rabbits.

Has rigid daily routine.

Should smile too much.

Will try any food.

Cannot resist waiting in lines.

Only has tighty-whitey underwear.

Buys shoes from nursing supply store.

Is best friends with old people.

Must have name tags sewn into his clothes with address
and phone number in case of an emergency.

Someone in the room then asked about meteorological understanding but I said no. It was important but not vital, not like these other qualities on the list. A guy could be whip-smart with meteorology skills but what's that got to do with being a weatherman? It's a little like saying a smart news reporter makes a great anchorman. Let's also consider the very real possibility that meteorology is nothing less than wizardry handed down to us from Arthurian times. Was Merlin the first weatherman? I don't think there's enough evidence to point to the contrary. If that's the case, then we have to assume that anyone who studies meteorology is really a wizard. I don't know about you but I think having a wizard on staff is not very professional. Is it neat? Of course it's way cool, but is it safe? Wizards are notorious for meddling in affairs they should not meddle in—using potions and spells in harmful ways and just generally engaging in mischief. In my opinion the safety issue outweighs the cool benefits of having a wizard around. I struck meteorology off the list and we went looking for our man.

The guys spread out, going to city parks, drinking fountains, bus stops, places where there were ducks—no stone was left unturned. Champ brought back a guy who on the surface looked pretty good, but when he was fully vetted it was discovered he had been working in a petroleum refinery and had been exposed to way too many gas leaks. Ed Harken found a timid-looking fortysomething man feeding bread crumbs to ducks out of an Aquaman lunch box but every time he tried to approach him the guy ran away like a scared deer. Brian just took off looking for tail and wasn't much help at all.

Turns out lady luck was with me again. She has always favored Ron Burgundy and I have honored her with many burning sacrifices. I found Brick Tamland sitting on a park bench listening to a baseball game through a tiny transistor radio. I knew he was our guy from the moment I saw him. I asked him about the game and lo and behold, he produced a turtle from his pocket and told me his name was "Turtle." The rest of the conversation went something like this:

**Brick**
**I have a head and feet too.**

**Me**
**What's that?**

**Brick**
**I am inside my head and outside my head.**

**Me**

**My name is Ron Burgundy.**

**Brick**

**My name is name.**

**Me**

**I'm a News Anchor.**

**Brick**

**I know one thing for sure. . . .**

**Me**

**What's that?**

**Brick**

**It's a funny sunny funny day.**

Truer words have never been spoken. In fact, since the very first days on record, there never has been anything but a sunny day in San Diego. Every day in San Diego is exactly the same as the day before. Here was the perfect guy. When I asked him where he lived his first response was to point at me and yell, "Stranger! Danger!" But when he saw I wasn't going anywhere he checked inside his elastic underwear band and read where it said "Brick Tamland, 410 Meadow Lane, San Diego, California, USA."

The man was a natural. He stood in front of a map and smiled and told everyone that today was sunny and tomorrow was also going to be sunny. He did fun segments with elementary school kids and old people. He went to petting zoos and raffled weather maps for charity, and every day he did the birthday list off the top of his head. Was he mentally challenged? Sure. Did we know it then? Of course not. We had mentally challenged people playing football, working in aviation, appointed secretary of agriculture. Mentally challenged folks taught high school shop, made excellent nurses and wrote television shows. It was a simpler time. Have we progressed since then? It's a good question. Brick Tamland is my friend and he's a retard.

With Brick in place we had it. We had the entire news team. Our domination in the San Diego area went unchecked for years. We were beyond legendary. We were gods. No statement of fact has ever been more factual than this one: We were the best news team that ever lived.

# THE NIGHT I MADE LOVE TO BRUCE LEE

Here's a quick story that I just have to tell. In 1973 martial arts champion and actor Bruce Lee came to San Diego to promote his new film, *Enter the Dragon*. I've always been a fan of the martial arts. I love the kicking and the flipping and the hitting. It really gets the heart pumping. I can't say I've mastered martial arts. I've taken karate classes and I do have a green belt. The problem for me is if I get into a fight I tend to improvise a lot. The karate goes out the window and I end up throwing O'Leary and Johnson around like a drunken idiot. I wish I were a karate expert like Bruce Lee. Sometimes I imagine myself in a situation with a briefcase full of important top secret documents and seven Asian guys have surrounded me in an attempt to steal the briefcase. I then pretend that I must fight them off using martial arts. I usually win, but not always.

I was a little nervous about meeting Bruce Lee because I am such a fan. His nunchuk work alone is simply legendary. Nunchuks, or "nunchaku," as the Chinese call them, are two sticks connected by a chain and used as a weapon in martial arts. If I'm in a room with nunchuks you might as well forget it. It's like putting down a plate of peanut butter cookies, I cannot resist picking them up. I will invariably grab those nunchuks and start flipping them around, whirling them through the air and within seconds my whole face is bruised and bleeding. I can't work 'em. I just can't. Don't even let me hold them. I will start swinging them all over the place and bonk. "Bonk" is the wrong word. You can't get taken to the hospital when you are "bonked." It's like a team of horses has trampled me.

So I go to meet Bruce Lee in the lobby of the Hilton in downtown San Diego. Sure enough, as soon as I'm seated across from him for an interview I notice the nunchuks. I remember reaching for them. I remember Bruce Lee smiling at me and the next thing I know I'm lying in a room at the Hilton with welts on my face. Those darn nunchuks! Apparently I hit myself five or six times in the head and then went down. Bruce Lee, the perfect gentleman, suggested I be taken to his room until I came to. When I finally regained consciousness it was well into the evening and frankly I was a little embarrassed to be lying in bed in his hotel room. It's not important to say it at all but the Hilton has the finest bedding, the best thread count and firmest pillows of any of the hotel chains. Oh, and the service is excellent.

When I came to, Mr. Lee was washing my feet in the tradition of a Japanese samurai warrior. It's traditional for the samurai to sponge the feet of honored visitors. I noticed that all my clothes had been removed. Mr. Lee was also naked—in the tradition of the samurai warrior. Humility, respect and hospitality are some of the traits of a true samurai along with courage, quickness and strength. Their ability to move gently and stay secretive, striking at the opportune moment, is a result of hours and hours of disciplined study. I respect these ancient Japanese warriors and their customs so when Mr. Lee explained to me in his broken, frankly awful English that he needed to make love to me, I understood the cultural significance. Historians tell us that the samurai warriors would seek out village men for a night of lovemaking before heading into battle. It was a great honor to be chosen thusly. I didn't know this historical fact at the time but Mr. Lee explained this to be the case. I pointed out that he was Chinese not Japanese but he brushed this aside saying it didn't really matter. Our eyes locked. He was, without a doubt, a beautiful man. The musculature alone was something to behold but the eyes were where he got you. Those dark pools were just too enchanting, like two warm baths, you could not but be enticed to take a dip. There was a part of me that wanted to look away but I knew that would be a sign of great disrespect.

The lovemaking was lightning quick, like his fighting style. His efficiency and flexibility were stunning. There were hands and feet all over the place. With all the biting and scratching it was like wrestling with three hairless wolves. Keep in mind this was 1973 and long before homosexuality was invented. I've made my stance pretty clear on how I feel about that and how I'm A-OK with the whole business but this had very little to do with anything of that nature—this was two warriors going at it with great respect and admiration for ancient traditions. Was there tenderness? Of course there was. Was it sexually gratifying? Yes. Did fingers find their way into places reserved for baser functions? You bet. But all of it happened in the fraternal spirit of male bonding, just like in olden times when men did stuff like that all the time. It was very manly.

When it was over we both felt the triumph of having worshipped at the altar of heroes. We were two proud warriors: he, the ancient Chinese samurai, and I, like some noble Greek champion of yore. We enjoyed a couple of cigarettes and lay next to each other in the quiet peace of a job well done. We were just a couple of guys.

As I left the room that morning he turned to me and said in his terrible English, "Mr. Burgundy, we like golden boat in river that have no current."

"Huh?" I said.

"My feewings to you are like night bird afwaid of light."

"You feel for me like a bat? Okay. See you."

I walked out never to see him again. He was to pass away two weeks later in Hong Kong. I miss Bruce Lee—he was a great fighter, a decent actor and a great lover. Anyway, that story gets told at least once a day, sometimes twice, to just about anyone I meet.

# MY LOVE FOR THIS COUNTRY

I don't often talk about it because I don't like to brag but I am a real patriot. It's a pretty controversial opinion, I know, but I love the United States of America and I'm not afraid to say it. There was a time, from about 1967 to 1974, when I would make phone calls to people I didn't know all across this land and tell them that I loved the United States. Imagine you're sitting in your home, lying in bed or in the kitchen enjoying a meal, and the phone rings. Now imagine picking up that phone and the first thing you hear is "I love the United States." It must have been great. My phone bills were through the roof! I didn't care. It was my way of giving back. Some guys went off to war, some gave to charities and still others had red, white and blue belts. I called people at any hour of the night in cities all across this nation to let them know how I feel.

If you don't love this country you need to go and spend a half an hour in Canada or Mexico. Here's two countries, literally right next to us, that really blew it. I get down to Mexico from time to time. San Diego is a just a short way from the border and it can be a fun day to drive down, hit Tijuana, take in a show, maybe watch a bullfight, and eat some tacos. I'll usually also have a drink or two. Here's what always happens. After the show, or the bullfight I'll have a couple more drinks. Well, that just about does it. The rest of the night is a circus blur of colorful piñatas and distorted toothless laughter. I don't know how it happens but somehow, after the bullfight or the show, I get drugged. It happens every time. Some sneaky Mexican puts something in my drink and good-bye, Ron Burgundy. How long am I out? Sometimes weeks. Ed Harken, my good friend and station manager at Channel 4, sent a team of navy SEALs into Mexico one time to see if he could find me. In the end they did find me but what they found was a surprise to all, including myself. I wasn't even Ron Burgundy. My name was Señor Big Jones and I was the mayor of a fishing village on the Baja Peninsula. I had been mayor for almost a month, establishing new literacy programs and public works projects, giving the town a real sense of pride. I worked like the devil, pushing through important legislation not just for well-heeled residents, of which there were none, but for the simple man in the street. I think I could have easily won a

second term—I had plans for a new light rail transit system—
but Ed had me airlifted back to San Diego and the town fell
back into the hands of the shitbird who ran it before. Maria,
my wife during this period (go figure!), tells me that the Big
Jones Library still stands, with one of the finest collections
of original incunabula in the world, including two complete
copies of the Gutenberg Bible, whatever the heck that is. Oh
well, I have been known to do some pretty dumb stuff when
I'm on a bender.

In general, and this is only part of the problem with the
country, Mexico is not a place to go on a bender. Apart from
my colorful time as a mayor and the year I was a hill bandit,
the usual Mexican bender ended with me in jail. Tradition-
ally I'd wake up and some squat *polistero* (Spanish for "po-
liceman") would be pointing his pudgy Mexican finger in my
face yelling something about me throwing punches. I don't
doubt it. I have thrown a lot of punches in Mexico. When
you get the whole news team down there, Brian, Champ and
Brick, you are talking about a human tornado of irresponsi-
ble fists. We don't go looking for fights, but gosh darn it, those
Mexican guys down there can't take criticism. I mean, you
open your mouth about how their food smells, or how they
speak American worse than children, or how there isn't one
of them with blond hair—reasonable and fair criticism—and
they just go crazy! Do I love Mayan art? Yes. Do I love Cortés?
Yes. Do I love Herb Alpert and the Tijuana Brass? Of course I
do. I love the Mexican peoples but they can be a proud, fiery
race. One theory, which I believe will one day be taken as fact,
explaining why their passion often outstrips their reason is

related to brain size. Due to a bean diet and other environmental factors, like their proximity to the sun and its powerful shrinking rays, their brains are just not that big. Has this theory been proven? No, but sometimes it's not prudent to wait for all the facts to come in. You have to quickly sign up for a theory so you can say, "I was there first."

There are many great things about Mexico. If it wasn't a huge waste of time a guy could write a whole book about Mexico. They got history. I mean, somebody made those pyramids, right? (I'm revealing stuff I said I never would, so I would prefer it if you read this next sentence after I'm dead. Those pyramids were built by aliens. That's a fact. The pyramids in Egypt were built by the British in the seventeenth century and the pyramids in Vegas were built by my good friend Steve Wynn. These are all facts. They are disputable for sure but facts just the same.) Mexico is very rich with history. If I were to write such a book, a gigantic waste of my time mind you, but if I were to write it I would bind it in sumptuous Corinthian leather and illustrate it with paintings by my very best friend, LeRoy Neiman. The book would weigh at least twenty-five pounds and would make a great addition to any fine library, and if you're into pressing flowers between the pages of books this would be the one. I have a book of poems by Henry Wadsworth Longfellow, the undisputed champion of American poetry, that I purchased in an old curio shop called B. Dalton for thirty-six dollars with beautiful etched illustrations and golden pages bound in the most expensive absolutely real leather available. It's probably a first edition and I own it. I make sure people see it and talk about it when they come in my house. You can't miss it. The display case I built for it makes it impossible to open the front door all the way but it's worth it. I'm sure this Mr. B. Dalton is pretty steamed I walked off with a first-edition Longfellow, our greatest poet, for thirty-six bucks! Guess what? He's not getting it back! Anyway, if I was to write a history of Mexico, meaning if I was willing to take time away from picking my nose or watching *Jeopardy!* or sitting on the toilet, it would be that kind of book—a big luxurious book with old-timey Spanish-style letters. I would call the book *The Fabulous Fables and Rich Tales of Olden Mexico and Its Regal Peoples.* I would like to see that title written in gold! I'm beginning to think I may just write this book. I bet everyone in Mexico would appreciate it—to have a book written specifically about you by a legitimately important American! Who wouldn't want that? The Mexicans may not deserve such a book but I'm going to give it some serious thought. Can you imagine waking up one morning in that godforsaken, dust-blown country and then hearing that Ron Burgundy has taken the time to write a book all about you and your land? Incredible. It would be incredible. I'm going to do it.

The fact is the United States of America is better than Mexico not for all the reasons above but for this simple fact: The Mexican people are THE most self-centered people I know. Here's a little test I throw at your average Mexican. I have five questions locked and loaded that I will spring on them just to prove my theory from time to time.

**Question 1.** Who signed the Declaration of Independence first?

**Question 2.** How many original colonies were there?

**Question 3.** Name three Hostess baked-good products.

**Question 4.** Order these five cities by population, highest to lowest: Toledo, Mobile, St. Paul, Salt Lake City, Orlando.

**Question 5.** Sing the national anthem.

As you can see, no tricks here, just plain simple questions anybody on this green earth should be able to answer, especially Mexicans. Notice I don't just ask culturally specific questions. These are questions to which everyone in the world knows the answer. Of course in this country children can answer these questions! In Mexico hardly anybody knows the answers. Who doesn't know the original colonies? Who can't say three Hostess products? Cupcakes! Twinkies! Ho Hos! Easy! It's not like I'm asking some poor Mexican guy off the street to recite the Constitution. Heck, *I* can't even do that. But really? You grow up a few miles from the greatest country in history and you don't even know "The Star-Spangled Banner"? That's either stupidity or willful ignorance. I go back and forth on this one. I used to only believe it was willful ignorance, which got me into a lot of fights and a lot of jail time. Now I see the Mexican as a simple man without much capacity for learning. It goes back to my theory on brain size. In some ways I feel sorry for him. As a great nation we should do something, but what? What can you really do if the people themselves don't want to learn American history so they can better themselves? What can you do! It's terribly frustrating! Goddamn it, I just threw my typewriter out the window! It gets me so frustrated though. You're not going to believe this; I threw another typewriter out the window. That's two that have flown through the air while I've been writing about Mexico. I gotta cool down. Typewriters are heavy and could cause a lot of damage down below. I took a shower. I shouldn't get so worked up. Anyway, I challenge you to find a nation wallowing in its own stupid patriotic pride more than the Mexican nation. Everywhere you go idiots are waving flags and bragging about how great they are. Okay, if you're so great, how is it you can't even sing the national anthem? Grrrrrr! Hard to believe but I threw out my last typewriter. Luckily Sears was open, where I have a card, and I was able to purchase THEIR last typewriter. No more writing about Mexico!

Canada is a whole different ball of wax. Imagine sitting in an airport lobby for three days. The only food you can eat is raw potatoes and water. The whole time you're being forced to listen to babies crying and the hits of Sha Na Na. Also there are no bathrooms. This is the kind of insufferable boredom one feels the moment you enter Canada. Your whole body begins to physically decay. The spiritual life drains out of you. Suicide constantly enters your thoughts. Being awake in Canada offers nothing more than watching the sands of your own mortality pass through the hourglass until it is empty. There is nothing to be hopeful about. There is no projection of something better, only existence in the rawest form.

A Canadian might tell you he is happy. Don't be fooled. He is living within a sickening paradigm that defines happiness as joyless existing devoid of those qualities that make us human. Almost any Canadian you meet in our country and who has been out of Canada for a while can tell you that he now lives in a magical land. That's why so many of the Canadians you meet in this country are so creative and pleasant. They have escaped a prison worse than any concentration camp ever constructed.

I've done news stories in Canada. I don't like to go there but sometimes duty calls. Within about five minutes of entering the country I start having suicidal thoughts. The prospect of death seems like a better alternative than being in Toronto or Vancouver. I usually start drinking, which is what the whole country does. They make their beer with a higher alcohol content so they can numb out the pain faster. Most of them don't drink beer though. Most of them drink gasoline. The Indians around Medicine Hat drink turpentine thickened with rat poison every night hoping they won't wake up in Canada the next day. Go there. You'll see. Of course, drinking is a two-edged sword. It can lead to great sadness. Combine that sadness with the naturally depressed state of everyday living in Canada and you will want to lie down on a railroad track. I have done this. I was covering the winter Olympic Games in Calgary. I was trying everything in the book to stay positive. I made sure I had friends around. I packed a pamphlet of daily affirmations, along with puzzles and games. I played flute every morning. I hung out in the ski lodge by the fire and read children's books to Baxter. But it was no use.

Slowly Canada worked its way into my bones. I lost focus. I was told to cover the women's biathlon, normally a very exciting sport with skiing AND rifle shooting and women, but I became more and more aware I was standing in Canada. My stomach became heavy, like I had eaten mud. My shoulders stooped. I lost any bounce to my step as I trudged through the snow. Life lost all meaning until a light of hope guided me. I followed the light, a beautiful blue ray, for what seemed like days. The light sang to me. It sounded like the voices of Karen Carpenter, Debby Boone and Olivia Newton-John combined into one welcoming, nurturing symphony. I was in a near-blissful trance and when I saw where it had led me I was euphoric. It was a railroad track. My escape from Canada was only a nap away. I lay down and fell asleep. Luckily for me a big Swede came along. The Swedish people have a great capacity for boredom. Although they are not boring themselves, they can withstand boring situations and boring people with great skill. The Swede took me to a McDonald's, where I was nursed back to believing I was in America. I stayed in the confines of those golden arches for a full week before I even had the courage to step out into Canada again. In the hundred or so steps I took to the helicopter that was waiting to take me to the United States and safety, I contemplated strangling myself.

Again, I don't want to disparage any Canadians here. Outside of their own country they can be simply delightful. I've met some very playful ones. I do however keep my guard up. If someone is introduced to me as a Canadian I instinctively fortify myself for the torrent of soul-crushing boredom to come plunging out of their mouth. I even cover my ears if I suspect them of not having been properly Americanized. I once had to interview singer-songwriter Joni Mitchell. She's from Canada. I very was hip to the new music scene and she was a real up-and-comer. Here's a transcript of the interview. Notice how quickly my mood changes.

**Ron**

**So tell me about this new brand of folk and rock.**

**Joni Mitchell**
**You know, it's hard to put a label on it.**

**Ron**
**Uh-hum.**

**Joni Mitchell**
**I think a lot of us, those of us who came out of the Troubadour up in L.A., consider ourselves songwriters first.**

**Ron**
**Uh . . .**

**Joni Mitchell**
**My good friend Carole King started out as just that—a songwriter. She really didn't have ambitions beyond that.**

**Ron**
**Please stop.**

**Joni Mitchell**
**I'm sorry.**

ABOVE: The Burgundy family, 1942. We didn't have much but we had each other. Unfortunately we hated each other. The boy in the dress is my brother Horner. BELOW: Is it wrong to say I was a very sexy baby? I know I felt it. How could that be wrong?

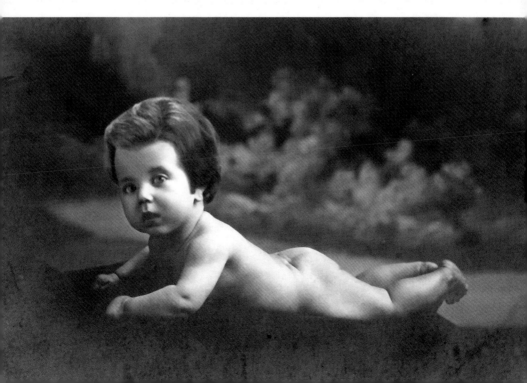

1958 graduating class of Our Lady Queen of Chewbacca High School.

My first sweetheart, Jenny Haggleworth.

Me, Miles and Bird at Pinky's Inferno, 1952. Had I not found this photographic evidence I'm not sure people would have believed me. Whew.

Brokaw with a double-breasted suit! The guy had a knack for beating me to the punch.

At the top of my game with Barbara and Walter. They were tons of fun when they stopped talking.

Sir Humphrey. The greatest gamecock that ever entered a cockpit.

Lucretia. My finest broadsword.

**Ron**

I'm trying. It's hard. So . . . go on. What else?

**Joni Mitchell**

Are you okay?

**Ron**

No. No I'm not okay. You are boring the shit out of me. Every word coming out of your mouth is like another pillow to my face, suffocating me to a cold mute death. STOP IT, RON! BE PROFESSIONAL! What's it like being a singer?

**Joni Mitchell**

I'm confused.

**Ron**

Answer the question! NO, DON'T! Pleeeeease don't answer the question. Come on, Ron! Be a professional. Whatsitlikebeingasinger?

**Joni Mitchell**

Um, well. I enjoy the intimacy of performance.

**Ron**

Stop it! I know what you're doing. You're trying to kill me. This woman is from Canada! WE HAD A RULE. WE HAD A RULE, DAMN IT! I CANNOT TAKE IT!

**Joni Mitchell**

What's going on? Should I sing something from my new album, *Clouds*?

**Ron**

**Lady. If you sing one note in this studio I will hang myself from the lights. Did you hear me? I will step up on this news desk, undo my tie and hang myself from the lights!**

What a laugh! Thankfully Joni Mitchell moved to the U.S. and settled with us here in Southern California, where she became more American and less Canadian. Her unorthodox chord changes and haunting voice frequently can be heard coming forth from the cassette deck I have in my bedroom. I've almost forgotten she is Canadian. No, I would say across the board when I was challenged with an interview of a Canadian talent, be it world-famous writer Margaret Atwood, funnyman Rich Little or rock musician Neil Young, I ended the interview always threatening to kill myself.

What is so surprising about this is that Canada, except for being colder and maybe having more pine trees and lakes, is basically the same, geologically speaking, as Minnesota or Michigan. It really should be as exciting and prideful as America. It just isn't. I mean, both Mexicans and Canadians can express pride in their respective countries but it's a false pride. It's like the kind of pride someone has in being a loser or an artist instead of a businessman. Everyone knows you wanted to be a businessman but then you became an artist. You have no choice but to take pride in it. That's just not the case with our great country. We are number one. We take great, truthful and honest pride in being number one.

Sometimes when I'm driving the freeways of San Diego I

will put on my national anthem tape. It has no words, just the music. I had the tape made for the day when I would be asked to sing the anthem before a World Series game. It hasn't happened yet, some sort of mix-up I'm sure, but when it does I will be ready. However, I've listened to our beautiful anthem thousands of times and I must say I've never liked the words. I've never felt they captured the true feeling of how much I love this country. Over the years I've played around with my own lyrics and I must say, should I ever get the chance to do the national anthem at a World Series, or anywhere for that matter, I would probably do my own new and better words. I almost hesitate to share it with you now because I just know it will get ripped off and then IT will become the new national anthem and I won't see a dime. Not that I'm in it for money, but you know.

My New National Anthem (To the tune of the old one. I'm very happy with the old tune.)

This is a great land,
with awesome majesty.
Nobody does it better
over land or even sea.
It's got all the right moves
for being the best.
You've got the cities in the East
and the mountains in the West.

The women here are gorgeous.
Not all of them but many.
It's got a lot of class,
from the dollar to the penny.
So make mine a double
and drinks are on the house.
For those who love their country
I am buying the next round.

Needless to say I'm pretty proud of this baby. It was a struggle but all poetry is pain sayeth the bard, right? I tend to get poetic when waxing on about my country. My love for the country knows no bounds. This land has given birth to the blues down in the deep delta, jazz born out of the struggles of the Irish immigrants who settled in Chicago, the hot dog, the old Mississippi rolling through the vast plains of Kansas and on down to Louisiana. America is the birthplace of Mark Twain, Oscar Wilde, Humphrey Bogart, the Dust Bowl, the Hollywood Bowl, the Super Bowl. Oh, greatest country! I love thee and thine thick pine forests and thundering trout streams. I love yine valleys wet with dew and sunshine, yine golden meadows glowing in light. Oh, Americans! What hath we if not heaven right here? 'Tis ours, this emerald isle, this blessed plot, this earth, this realm, this America! I care not for vainglorious arrows that sling at me, nor do I care wenst they came. I am impervious to all mettlesome darts and such. I am an American. My name is Ron Burgundy and that, my good friends, is an American name.

# WHAT'S WRONG
# WITH AMERICA?

Okay, so you know my feelings for this country I call home. It is the second-finest country in all of the Americas. However, just because I love this land with more fierce love than my love for Veronica Corningstone, my wife, it does not mean I cannot be critical. For example, I'm in love with myself but it doesn't stop me from occasionally staring into my thirty-foot floor-to-ceiling mirror and saying to myself, "Ron, you could lose a few pounds." Criticism is a form of self-love the way I see it. We live in troubling times when criticism is seen as unpatriotic. There are a lot of red-faced blockheaded anchormen out there calling themselves newsmen who wrap themselves in patriot colors to hide the fact that they cannot handle reasonable adult criticism. This is an alarming trend the way I see it. The job of an anchorman is not to lecture the viewers on patriotism but to read the teleprompter as soberly as possible and let them decide what is right or wrong. To be honest you can really stretch the limits of sobriety and still achieve this goal. I've always had a nip or two before I go on. I usually have a few during the broadcast. My whole team enjoys drinking throughout the day. When I was at Channel 4, Ed Harken, the station manager, would have loud screaming meetings about being "over budget." People would pound their fists and raise their voices and stand on chairs and throw typewriters. It was a real sight but no one could ever figure out where the money went. Was it suits? Was it hair and makeup? Massage chairs? Fireworks? Archery equipment? Then one day some bold intern from Stanford University yells out, "It's the booze." Sure enough, over half our monthly budget was going to alcohol! That intern was fired immediately and I hope never works in news again. My point being, it doesn't take much to get the job right. Anyway, I will venture some well-thought-out criticism of this country and hope to God you idiots don't accuse me of being unpatriotic.

Our babies have gotten uglier. I don't know why this is but you can't deny it's happening. Is it inbreeding? Is it high levels of newfangled foodstuffs like yogurt and lettuce? Who knows? There is just no answer out there, but look around, babies are not cute anymore. Women seem to not notice it as well because often they become emotionally attached to their babies. It can ruin my whole day—some proud and delusional woman will shove her terrifyingly ugly thing right in my face and I am made to scream. It's just about at epidemic proportions. If it keeps going at this rate none of us will want to go outside by the year 2015 for fear of seeing a disgusting-looking infant. If women are going to keep having these gross little meatballs I think we need to start thinking about social engineering of some kind. Calm down. Not Nazi-type stuff here but just simple common sense. We could set up a tribunal of judges and decide which babies need to be shipped off to England, where there have never been good-looking babies. We could have this whole country looking beautiful and fresh in no time. I would say Thai babies can get a pass. I've never seen an ugly Thai baby. Never. We should as a nation be encouraged to breed with people from Thailand. It could solve everything.

I'm sick and tired of people driving too slow in the left lane. It just has got to stop, plain and simple. A few years back I was racing to a strawberry festival outside of San Diego up in the Laguna Mountains when I encountered a tan Honda Civic rolling along in the left lane. The driver had effectively set up a roadblock for those of us wanting to pass. I calmly waited for an opportunity but after about thirty to forty seconds of this bullshit I came down on my horn. I stayed on that horn for easily ten minutes and this guy just wasn't budging. All I could do was laugh. You gotta take these things in stride and live and let live. I relaxed and settled into the speed this guy apparently decided we all should drive. I bided my time like a Zen Buddhist until he slowly got in the other lane and slid off the highway. Well, I wasn't going to let this guy off

that easy. I followed him down the ramp, turned the corner
with him and drove on through several small towns around
the outskirts of San Diego. When he stopped for cigarettes at
a 7-Eleven I parked a half a block away and carefully waited
for this joker to get back into his car. We rode on through the
rest of the day, me following him ever so craftily. Finally he
pulled up to a typical dumb shit suburban house with a little
picket fence and some kids' bikes on the lawn. Oh boy, now
was my chance! I waited a few hours until the sun went down
and took out my gallon can of paint thinner. I scurried up to
his car in the moonlight and drenched the car from the hood
to the trunk with the paint thinner, then I lit it on fire. I left
this note on the grass for him. It read: "Dear asshole, I want
to thank you for making me miss the strawberry festival with
your selfish and asinine driving. You are the worst person I
have ever encountered and know that I am watching you. If
you ever sit in the left lane again for any reason other than
passing I will burn your house down and hopefully you in it!
Ron Bu." I started to sign it but then I thought differently.
Years later I found out I was suffering from something called
"road rage" and it's a real medical thing! I'm still mad at the
guy to this day but my actions were way inappropriate and I
know that now. There have been so many advancements in
human psychology.

College! This country has gone college crazy! Everyone
and their dog has to go to college. If you make it through
high school and you don't go to college, then you are an out-
cast. Well, this is ridiculous! I think we should go back to the
good old days when nobody went to college except for homely

women and pasty rich white guys from Boston. What's wrong with making birdhouses for a living? You don't need college to lay tar on a roof. Is there a better job than laying tar on a roof? You play around with hot tar, you're outside with your buddies cracking dirty jokes and then you head to the bar for some icy cold beers. Is college gonna get you that? Nope. Here's what college will get you: a sad, lonely, competitive longing for unattainable goals and a deep anxiety about impending failure and finally death. Studies show you will also get herpes.

People need to treat me with more respect. It should be a foregone conclusion that I am treated with the utmost respect, but there are people out there in my own country who don't respect me and that's just un-American. I know I said I wouldn't wrap myself in the flag like every other ham-headed idiot on TV today but frankly speaking, if you don't respect me then you are a terrorist. It's pretty simple. The government can stop the spying on its own people. All they need to do is make up a list of people who don't respect me and put them in Guantánamo Bay until they can make them respect me. I'm not completely serious of course, but really I am.

Let me tell you what else we got wrong in this country, and that's the whole gun situation. There are too many guns out there and not enough people. The gun-to-people ratio is like five guns to every person on the earth. That ratio is all wrong. At the very least there should be ten thousand people for every gun. By my calculations that means we need at least one hundred billion people. Let's start making more people to catch up with the gun population. Making people is easy.

You put your penis in a vagina and wiggle it around. Done. I've made a lot of people that way. A lot. Wait, no I haven't. You wouldn't be able to prove it anyway.

Another complaint I have is the way we treat the gays. Well, I don't like it! As you know, for the most part I'm a heterosexual man who likes to put my parts into ladies' holes. (There may have been a classier way to say that.) I think maybe I was born this way and apart from the few times when the situation got the best of me, like the aforementioned Bruce Lee incident, I have not desired romantic and sexual encounters with other men. In the seventies I ended up in a lot of hot tubs with all kinds of hands and feet groping around underneath the water. You can't keep track of all those hands and feet. You just can't. Did some guys go for my wiener? I have no idea and I don't care. It was good clean fun. (Just a little side note on the "clean" part: In '78 I donated my own hot tub to the prestigious Boston College of Medicine, where it still remains today as a source for the world's largest collection of streptococcus.) Apart from some drunken and good-time fun with a few guys, I would say I'm pretty sure of my sexual orientation. Now, on the other hand there are some guys who are made different than me. They are gay guys, or if you are in the science community you might call them homosexuals. They were made that way—just the way I was made to use my penis for entering vaginas and such. (NOTE: Think up a more scientific way to say this for final draft of book.) Honestly a gay man living his gay life in a gay way out in the world as a gay is a more courageous man than most of the straight men I know. That goes for gay ladies as well. The good news is this country has become more and more accepting of gays over the last thirty years and I've come along with it. I'll admit it, it wasn't easy for me to find out Paul Lynde was gay. That was a shocker. Then I got hit with George Takei and I was like, "George Takei? Is everyone gay?!" But then I started to think to myself, "Ron, what do you care if Lynde or Takei is gay?" Were they happy hiding it? Did I feel better living in a world where people had to hide who they were because of fear? Is our country that afraid? I hope not. Sure, there are some tobacco-faced old meatheads who take to the airwaves or dried-up old prunes or rabid young conservatives who are afraid of change, but why should they ruin it for the rest of us? I hate change too. I wish baseball was still a sport. I would like to see a return to bigger phones. I miss Burt Lancaster pictures. Whatever happened to MTV?

Let me tell you a story about a four-year-old boy playing with his new slingshot in his backyard in Iowa. The boy got pretty good at it. He could hit cans fifty feet away. He could hit tree branches and street signs. Well one day he took aim at a bird seventy-five feet away and he hit it. The bird fluttered and fell from the tree. The boy was elated. He killed a bird with his slingshot! He was a great shot. He ran over to it and there it was on the ground. It didn't move and wasn't going to move ever again. It had no future. It was that easy; the boy had stopped it from being a bird. He thinks about that mockingbird every day. I'm as conservative as the next guy when it comes to suits and cocktails, but not letting a gay guy be who he is is sort of like killing a mockingbird. That's my opinion on the gays.

———————

Other than those few things I would say our country is perfect. Sure, you could complain about Wall Street hoodlums stealing our pensions and inflating our real estate, which I do in a later chapter; you could whine about oil prices going through the roof and athletes hopped up on steroids. If you wanted to you could complain about the toxic amount of food we eat and the decline of the public school system. The cost of higher education is going through the roof. Children are spending too much time on gadgets. That's gotta have some sort of effect on something and it makes for good complaining. I like to complain about the fact that there are not enough horse pictures at the movie houses anymore. The three-piece suit is nearly extinct and no one seems to care! These days bartenders often forget a drink on the house. There's been a dangerous backlash against polyester. There needs to be more shows like *Night Court* on television. If I see any more tattoos I'm going to go berserk. You could wake up every morning and start complaining, but then you would just sound like the "News Anchors" on cable news today. No, we live in the third-greatest country in the world and we should be pretty proud of it. I know I am. I wouldn't mind it if there were a few less old people.

# WHAT KIND OF BREATH TURNS A WOMAN ON?

Hot breath on a woman's neck and face is an aphrodisiac. That's a scientific fact that researchers have proven—not that I needed some Murgatroyd with a lab coat to tell me that a hot, humid whisper delivered inches from a woman you've just met in an elevator or on a buffet line can often seal the deal without the usual handwork. The secret, however, is not in the force of the exhale or the distance; no, the secret is in the breath itself. What kind of breath turns a woman on? I've made a bit of a study of this over the years and here are my top seven food combinations for effective hot breath. There's just no way these won't work. Let's say you're a hairy little man,

like an Armenian or a Greek, and on top of that you have one
of those dog faces common among Slavic people and Corsi-
cans. To further complicate matters you're sweaty and your
penis looks like a burnt marshmallow in a bird's nest. You,
my friend, are a big zero, but fear not; this hot breath stuff
will work! Not every time. Sometimes it will have the opposite
effect of what you're going for. Here's my list of recipes for effective sensual breath.

### RECIPE 1: "THE DRIED-UP RIVERBANK"

Thick, musty, lonesome and dangerous, that's the smell
and feeling of a dried-up riverbank. Women are terrified and
turned on by it. How to capture it all in a breathy whisper?
Simple. Shrimp dipped in stale beer and hot mayonnaise. Let
it sit in your mouth for no less than five minutes; work it into
your teeth. This one works from a long way out. Try it in a
room full of women and see if any react—more than likely
those who do won't be classy but they'll be moved by a memory long since buried that only the rancid smell of dried mud
can recover. If that memory is a pleasant one—and often it is
not—you are in business, my friend.

### RECIPE 2: "THE FOREIGN ELEMENT"

If you've ever been to Europe, which I have, five times for
pleasure, then you know the smell of a European café. It's absinthe and rich tobacco with a hint of an old-world standing
urinal. It's a delicious smell that when delivered the right way
can turn a frozen ice queen into a nonstop volcanic eruption
of hot love fluids. But who's kidding who? Absinthe is expen-

sive. Here's a way to get that same scent in your mouth on a budget. Take an onion. Let it sit in an open can of motor oil overnight. Put it in a blender with stale cigarettes and coffee grounds and drink. Voilà! European bar. If you can whisper a few words of French, like *mise en scène*, or gently sing an Edith Piaf song a few inches from her nose, that adds an extra element of continental spice. Some women find this irresistible. Others resist it, but stay with it; they give in eventually.

### RECIPE 3: "THE EARTHY GARDENER"

Cabbage, broccoli, beans and raw bacon. This one is about timing. Once this hits your gut you have about fifteen minutes to go to work before the farts set in. I would describe the smell as "stomachy dirt," like blowing a fan through compost. I've had some luck with loose women with the Earthy Gardener, but then they were pretty loose, so it's hard to say if it really works. Give it a try! Treat every day like a prison break!

### RECIPE 4: "SEVEN-CHEESE SAMURAI"

Just as it says. You eat seven different cheeses. Any kind will do but make sure you're eating at least a pound total. This one poses its own challenges. Women smell it coming from a mile away, making it harder to get in tight for real close breathing unless you employ the tactics of the samurai warrior. You need to keep your breathing to a minimum. Bring your heart rate down to a legally dead state. It helps to be hiding in a dark corner or under a desk or behind a filing cabinet. You must not move at all until the woman is absolutely within close range. Then the sleeper awakens and blows . . .

seven cheeses right at her face! It's a winner. Believe me. It has an effect.

### RECIPE 5: "THE ROADKILL"

Find some roadkill and eat it. I haven't even tried this one but I know it would work. I just know it. Let me know if you do try it. It's gotta work.

### RECIPE 6: "THE ANIMAL LOVER"

Who hasn't seen a beautiful woman come to her knees at the sight of a cute puppy? Oh how I've envied that puppy from time to time. Sometimes the envy gets to the point of really pissing me off. I remember a cute little basset hound puppy in particular who stole the attention of a woman I was interested in pursuing. I was as steamed as I ever get. I waited for the lady to get out of earshot and I laid into that puppy with every curse word my mouth could make. I hate curse words in general but that little dog got two earfuls that day! I had to lift the little guy's ears just to scream my anger right into his little dog head. Somewhere out there in the world there is a basset hound walking around with some very real psychological issues. I hope he eventually got some therapy. I'm really a friend to dogs, just not when they get between me and my own animal desires. Anyway . . . what is it about dogs that gets the ladies? Can't be their looks, because most dogs look like a pork roast with eyeballs. (Please, Baxter, do not read this!) Anyway I realized women love dogs because of their breath. "Eat a bowl of dog food, Burgundy," I said to myself one night, and so I did, and sure enough it was like cheating. Women go nuts for dog breath. (As an aside I should mention women in their late twenties really go for baby's breath. That's just a biological fact. I tried to find this breath—I ate jars and jars of baby food, cans of sweetened baby milk, even asked a woman to pump some breast milk for me, but no luck! You just can't get baby's breath unless you literally get a stomach transplant from a baby! Who would allow you to do that? I've befriended some very suspect "doctors" in my day but I doubt a one of them would feel comfortable replacing my stomach with a baby's stomach! Oh well, lucky babies! Sex appeal is wasted on the young!) When it comes to dog food I go right for the hard nuggets right out of a forty-pound bag. A handful will do you for the night. Word to the wise: If you're stealing the food from your own dog, be sneaky. Baxter put it together over several weeks that I had been taking his food and he confronted me directly. It was not pretty. We argued. Then he waited until I went to sleep and he bit my foot. He later told me he was so mad he would have bitten my face if it weren't for the fact that my face feeds us both. What a dog!

### RECIPE 7: "THE EXECUTIVE"

Well, here it is, my favorite and a sure winner. I don't leave the house without the Executive because it's just a no-nonsense heavy breath that when gently whispered into any woman's face will drive her nuts. Sardines and an old cigar. Yep, it's that simple. I keep a tin of sardines and half a stale cigar in my inside vest pocket at all times. The cigar provides the weight and the sardines provide the spice. It's like a gentle breeze blowing over a garbage truck, just enough to say, "I'm here and you are in for a heck of a night . . . a heck of a night!"

## MY NEIGHBOR: NEW DEVELOPMENTS

Just an update on the whole war I'm having with my neighbor Richard Wellspar. He borrowed my leaf blower and didn't return it. Baxter and I snuck into his backyard and I did indeed empty out my two garbage cans into his pool. The whole operation went off without a hitch. Baxter is a true professional. The next morning, who do you think is standing at my front door? Yep, Richard Wellspar, idiot! So he very calmly asks me if I know anything about the garbage in his pool. Well, I'm nothing if I'm not fast on my feet. I've spent a whole lifetime in the news game, where you have to be on top of it at every minute. I looked him square in the face and said, "It's not mine and I didn't do it." He looked confused. He showed me a wet Publishers Clearing House letter addressed to me. I was caught off guard for a second. Of course, all of the junk mail had my address on it! Ooooh boy, that was not smart. Baxter should have said something! Anyway, I came back at him with this: "Richard, here's the deal. This is something you should know about this neighborhood. You've only been here a few years, so how could you be expected to know this? Also you are a pool salesman or something and this kind of stuff is outside of your area of expertise. I'm a newsman, so I know just about everything. There are feral cats around here and they will take garbage cans and throw them in pools. Pretty standard stuff, really." He just said, "Okay, Ron. By the way, I am a money manager. I'm not a pool salesman." Then he walked away. Once again, nothing about the leaf blower! Incredible! I am beside myself.

# THE BIG TIME,
# OR WHEN I KNEW
# I HAD MADE IT

My face is buried in a wine-soaked pillow. Slowly my left eyelid lifts to reveal a dark corner of the room. There's a naked body there slumped over itself, sleeping, maybe dead. Stale wine fills my nostrils. I take it in and it feels safe. I know that smell and I like it. I like what it says about my current predicament. I'm too brain-soaked to move fast. I say to myself, "Take it in, Ron. Enjoy the mystery." Something weighs on my leg. It's hefty, like the stale wine smell in the room. . . . Hold up . . . wine smell? Is this a distillery? Did I pass out in a distillery? I've passed out in distilleries before. It doesn't look like a distillery, although I've been in some inventive distilleries. People make distilleries out of anything—toilets, gas pumps, refrigerators, showers, swimming pools. My dear old friend Gus Cranshaw operated a distillery out of a converted mail truck. He painted it up to look like the current mail trucks you see today and me and him would drive around Dallas picking up mail and reading it while stoned on "Cranshaw's Crazy Juice." That was Dallas in the late fifties. You could get away with stuff like that then. It was a lawless town.

Cranshaw was an aeronautical engineer with a Ph.D. from Stanford but by the time I met him he had lost 90 percent of his thinking capacity—still a hoot, just had no ability to reason. It didn't matter because almost all of the mailmen in Dallas in the fifties were slower people and alcoholics. Reports of mail theft were common. I went back to Dallas in '71 to do a puff piece on Roger Staubach. Cranshaw was alive and well but he only had about fifty words left to his vocabulary. As the newly elected postmaster general for the greater Dallas–Fort Worth area he was asked to speak frequently and he confided in me that it was no easy task. Somehow he had retained the word *thermal*, either from his days at Stanford or maybe from his work on his distillery, and with only fifty words to work with the word *thermal* came up often, as in "I smell a thermal coming," "Look at that thermal," "We got us a thermal," "Us thermal look good, thermal." He was later elected six times to the state legislature with the slogan "We gonna go thermal!" . . . Back to my current predicament. Maybe there's a body decomposing? Is it fermenting flesh?

I know that smell, mold mixed with infection and dead skin. Am I in the Tarantula's Lair again? Is this Venezuela? A moment of fear surges through my usually calm disposition. For one second I am paralyzed with heart-stopping terror. Horrendous memories strike at me like coiled snakes jumping at my face, but just as quick I fight them off. No, Ron, those days are over. Look around the room. There are no guns, no cameras, no demonic symbols painted on the wall. You play it safe now. Cool down and take it easy. . . . Maybe I'm in some kind of whorehouse. It's too small for a whorehouse. Stop guessing! Slow it down, Ron. Slow it down. Let the mystery unfold. Back to the weight on my leg. I can feel the smooth skin on my haunches. It's sensual. Hello, Mr. Hammersmith (one of the many names I give my penis). He has awakened, bloated with wine and memory and possibility. "Now is not the time for you," I say out loud. It may be the place but it is not the time. I will admit, Mr. Hammersmith has no real sense of time or space. He's his own agent, bound to no rules made by man. Nature is Mr. Hammersmith's lawgiver and even she grants him free rein within her strict code. For I have witnessed Mr. Hammersmith defy nature many times, taunting her with his insolence like Odysseus yelling back at Cyclops, full of hubris. Mr. Hammersmith has thus taunted nature with many unnatural acts and yet Mother Nature loves her impish man-child. I envy Mr. Hammersmith. He's not bound to reason. I'm talking about my penis, Mr. Hammersmith. No, he's an epicurean all the way. His morning bloat is pure joyful defiance! He's a rascal and I love him for it!

Unfortunately I have a head—a head filled with brain cells—and I am intrigued by the mystery that surrounds me. What is that weight on my leg? Do I have the muscle control to lift my head and look or should I continue to sleuth it out like the newsman that I am? It's a female leg. I'm fairly certain of that, although there are men who shave their legs. World-class swimmer and nine-time Olympic gold medalist Mark Spitz shaves his legs to lose the aquadynamic drag that body hair might cause in the water. I asked him one time in a candid on-air interview if he felt more like a woman without the hair. He didn't know how to respond to the question so I rephrased it like this: "Does shaving your legs make you feel sexy, more feminine?" Again, he laughed but did not understand what I was getting at. Here is a transcript of my interview with Mark Spitz from that point on.

**Ron**
**Come on, man.**

**Mark Spitz**
**Are you serious?**

**Ron**
**I'm an anchorman with sterling credentials.**

**Mark Spitz**
**You want to know if shaving my legs for my sport makes me feel more like a woman?**

**Ron**
**Does it?**

**Mark Spitz**
You're an idiot.

**Ron**
I would think it would go a long way to putting you in touch with your feminine side. Do you wear dresses ever? Maybe a wig?

[Long stare-down]

**Ron**
Are you not comfortable with wanting to be a woman?

[Something begins to agitate Mr. Spitz]

**Ron**
I've seen men up in San Francisco in heels and dresses that I swear to God you would think are women. I did. I thought they were women.

[Mr. Spitz nods his head]

**Ron**
I don't know if that's something you're interested in but I should warn you—you can shave your legs and put on heels and the prettiest dress in the world but you'll never even come close to what these men look like. They basically are women.

[Spitz looks off camera, confused]

**Ron**
Hey! Over here. This isn't Howard Cosell lobbing soft-

**balls at you, kid. This is San Diego and I am Ron Bur-
gundy. Answer the question! Does shaving your legs make
you feel like a woman? America wants to know!**

**[Spitz walks off set]**

It was one of the few times I lost my cool on camera but
gosh darn it, from time to time I let my insatiable need to
know get in the way of decorum. I respect the NEWS just too
much not to give a damn, and frankly he was hiding something. After the broadcast I ran after him. He took off like he
was afraid of somebody or something but I gave good chase.
I was fast on his heels all the way to the Coronado Bridge
but then—again, maybe because something scared him—he
dove into the harbor and at that point I threw up my hands
in comic defeat. I laughed so all of San Diego could hear me.
I certainly was not going to catch nine-time gold medalist
Mark Spitz in the water! It made for a good story.

At any rate it couldn't have been Mark Spitz's leg draped
over my own, that's for sure. This was before his time. More
likely a beautiful woman. That would make all the sense in
the world. Really quite simple: a night of drinks, maybe an
after-hours gentlemen's club, a dip in someone's pool if we
could find one driving around, a stroll through the natural
history museum, a private party and then to bed, where Mr.
Hammersmith could go to work in all his glory. How many
nights have gone like this—every one of them special in its
own way? How many times did I awake to this same sweet
scene played out like a jazz flute solo with infinite variations
on the same chords? I could almost describe the room be-

fore my eyes fully opened. There would be women, more than one, lying naked, and empty bottles and clothes hither and thither thrown about in passion's full fury. There might also be a half-eaten steak sandwich and some deviled ham. There could even be a fan of mine—a total stranger who had won a contest or something, "A Night on the Town with Ron Burgundy." The tales he or she would tell for the rest of his or her life! It was one of the ways I gave back and also it was one of the ways to get the station to pay for my nights on the town. In those days, '65, '66, a night on the town could run you three to four dollars, which was a good chunk of your paycheck. Newsmen were expected to party. Not like socialites and movie stars but like oilmen and footballers. There was a code amongst the real newsmen. You couldn't report the news till you paid your dues, and by *paying dues* I mean you had to outdrink and out-screw everyone else in the game. The code was a lifestyle and no one could outdo me. I was simply the best. I once went to have cocktails with Lana Cantrell and Bubba Smith. We agreed to meet in the Marina for a few afternoon drinks. I remember ordering something silly like a Naughty Squirrel. I was feeling zesty. I can remember the first sip. The next thing I felt was a boot to my rib cage. I woke up. I was in downtown Laramie with no pants, holding on to a bag of hundred-dollar bills. Another victory for sure. I know today people might look back and say, "Ron, you were an alcoholic."

Where was I? Oh yes, so I had regained consciousness in a strange small room with a naked or dead person in the corner and a female leg straddling my own leg. It was time to put on my thinking cap. First off, and this is something I do every morning to this day, I asked myself, are there any open wounds or bruises? I always like to assess the damage if there is any. Nope. I was feeling pretty good, maybe a bite mark on my arm but that hardly constitutes a problem. I noticed something gooey on my hand—a gooey substance. I knew I would have to sniff it but that could wait. I also noticed a sound. It was snoring, loud, contented snoring from a man. Aha! Besides the girl and the person in the corner there was someone else in the room with me. I tried to remember the evening. Was there another man with me, perhaps from the news team? We news people tend to celebrate in groups. If you get a bunch of us together, say at a conference, or maybe a big story brings the network affiliates into town, it's Katie, bar the door! Heck, Dan Rather and I aren't even allowed in the Flamingo hotel in Vegas anymore. That was a case where things got out of hand—unpaid bills, property damage, assault charges, etc. If it weren't for Rather's connection to the mob I don't think we would have left Vegas alive that night.

Rather is one of the best in the business. That is a fact I'm not afraid to report. With that smooth Texas drawl and that sexy I-will-mess-up-your-face-if-you-so-much-as-lay-a-hand-on-me smile, he is one classy operator. I've always said if I get caught in a Moroccan back alley and I'm looking at an all-or-nothing knife fight, Dan Rather or Charles Kuralt would be my pick for wingman. Both of these guys are as comfortable with a blade in their hand as a monkey is with his penis. Kuralt is legendary for quick-handed jabs and slashes, whereas Rather is the natural-born descendant of Gentleman Jim Bowie. He could toss a knife into a charging bear at fifty feet. I saw him do it one time back when bearbaiting was still very close to being legal. A man's bear got loose from his chains and headed into the crowd. Rather happened to be there on a story about Ross Barnett, the governor of Mississippi. Barnett was a big bearbaiting fan and an old-school racist. He had the Freedom Riders thrown in Parchman Farm, where they were strip-searched and humiliated. He said this about Bobby Kennedy:

"I say to you that Bobby Kennedy is a very sick and dangerous American. We have lots of sick Americans in this country but most of them have a long beard. Bobby Kennedy is a hypocritical, left-wing beatnik without a beard who carelessly and recklessly distorts the facts."

The bear headed straight for Governor Barnett and Rather dropped him like a sack of old beef. I asked Dan about it a couple of years later. I knew him to be a lefty from way back when we both were members of the Commie Party for a couple of weeks. He said, "I didn't want that bear to make a martyr out of that sack of shit." Rather could swear up a storm but I'll save that for later (see chapter 8).

Well, it was coming to me. The whole setup started to make sense. There had been a big story in San Diego that week.

The minor-league San Diego Padres became a Major League Baseball team and it was a huge, huge story! All the big network affiliates were in town. Every newsman—Mudd, Reynolds, Cronkite, Reasoner, Wallace, Huntley, Brinkley— they were all in San Diego to cover the story. So here's what must have happened. We got our stories in and then, because San Diego is my town, I hosted the evening. I took the whole

gang out to my favorite watering holes. I'm sure one thing led
to another and here I was in a small room with a contest winner, a naked woman or two and another man. All that was left
was for me to sit up and survey the room to see who'd survived
the night. I did just that. I sat up. My head hit something and
I immediately saw that I was in the cabin of a small schooner.
Sure enough Walter Cronkite, America's most trusted news
source, was snoring away in a hammock three feet from me.
His beard was maybe four or five days old. The person in the
corner was Korean, a sixty- or seventy-year-old woman (still
breathing thankfully), and the woman lying across me, sans
undergarments, was none other than a young Barbara Walters. A slow smile formed.

Here I was, the boy from Haggleworth, Iowa, in a boat,
drifting aimlessly at sea with two of the greatest newsmen who
ever lived. (There's always been some confusion over whether
to call a woman in the news business a "newswoman" or the
more proper "female newsman." If she's risen to the level of
a Barbara Walters, then she damn well deserves to be called
a "newsman." The end.) I took in the greatness of this important scene. How did I get here? Not the nuts and bolts of
how I got on the boat—Cronkite stole the boat off the harbor
pier, yelling, "I'm the greatest sailor that ever lived! I'm better than Sir Francis Drake! And that's the way it is!" And off
we went. We were four hundred miles off the coast when I
woke up. Weeks later we ended up in the Solomon Islands
on a remote outcropping, shipwrecked, because Cronkite is
NOT the greatest sailor that ever lived. Two months on that
island with those three people fighting off monitor lizards is

a whole other story. What I'm really getting at is clearly I had reached the pinnacle of success. I was number one in San Diego. Soon I had just put together the news team that would come to dominate that town for nearly a decade and I had just spent a night or maybe a week of lovemaking with Barbara Walters . . . and most likely Walter Cronkite and the old Korean woman, but let's focus on Walters. I can hardly think of a more prestigious honor than a night of wine-soaked sex with two respected newsmen like Cronkite and Walters. That morning, with nude bodies spread out in the cabin and the smell of body fluids everywhere, was the moment I realized I had made the big time.

It's no big deal but I'm taller than the guys on the team. I look shorter because I'm kneeling down. If you look, you can tell that my knees are bent. Clearly I'm not standing straight.

ABOVE: I'll be honest, Jackie O gave me the creeps. She looks like Jeanne Tripplehorn though. I'm wishing she was Jeanne Tripplehorn in this picture. No that's stupid. Tripplehorn was three years old when this photo was taken. BELOW: Norman Mailer was a real puss and I enjoyed beating him at everything.

Mark Eaton, Utah Jazz.

My great friend who I never shut up about, Lance Bullwright.

Ancient dinosaurs like the Tyrannosaurus rex terrorized the first
Mexican peoples.

ABOVE LEFT: Having a whale of a time! (I put that in here for laughs because of the word "whale" and there's a real whale in the picture. I've always liked jokes.) ABOVE RIGHT: My favorite bird of prey, Lady Samantha Hutchinson. BELOW: God's majesty knows no bounds.

ABOVE: Pointing at something. BELOW: Caught in the bubble! I go to jail for an $80 billion real estate mix-up. I've done longer stretches for public urination. Only in America!

ABOVE: Baxter refuses to get a job but I still love him. BELOW: My wife. My lover and a damn fine woman anchorman.

# MY TWELVE RULES FOR LIVING THROUGH A PRISON RIOT

Prison riots are boisterous affairs. You really want to try to avoid them if you can, but at one time or another you can just bet you'll be in the middle of one. I've been in eight of them. Three in this country and another five in various countries around the world. I've even started them! Here are my twelve rules for living through it.

**RULE NUMBER 1:** Use it now. If you're not an idiot, then you've spent your time in jail wisely, making weapons. You should have at the very least a zip gun, a carved wooden shiv, a broken-glass-covered soap ball, a garrote wire and a chair leg with some rusty nails in it. A lot of guys will have more than this but if you have these few simple tools you'll be okay. The key here is to recognize this is the moment to use these things. It's a not a collection to take pride in and show the other guys. Prison is not a craft fair. You made these things to hurt other people, so get to it!

**RULE NUMBER 2:** Look for weakness. There's always fear in the air. You might as well accept it and embrace it. Some men can't handle it. They buckle under the fear. These are the ones you need to attack. Hit them fast and hard and often and if they get back up, then you didn't do something right. Hitting a weaker man will gain you confidence when you have to go after the really big cats.

**RULE NUMBER 3:** Use a verbal assault. Different theories abound here. Do you come across as more fearful without talking? Are a few choice words all you need? The scariest man I ever came across inside or outside of prison was a man who could squish a human head in a fight and all he ever said was, "I'm going bananas!" He didn't open his mouth for any other reason but to say those words, and if he was saying those words, it was too late, my friend! So sometimes a man of few words can indeed be a terrifying thing. However, I like to yell out a torrent of threats while running right at my victim. You should practice these in your cell at night. Practicing lines with your cell mate is fun and helps pass the time. "Here comes the face eater" is a good one. I've also said this:

"I will rip your balls off and sauté them in garlic butter with basil and ground pepper. I will then add a garnish of shaved orange peels and a side of fresh-cut sliced beets misted with lemon juice. I will beautifully plate it and enjoy a glass of white wine with it while dressed in a tuxedo. It will be a Michelin three-star meal and you will not be invited to join me! Do you understand?"

**RULE NUMBER 4:** Go naked. Take your clothes off as soon as possible. It adds to the insanity of the whole scene. When watching scratchy security tapes of the riot later it's always a moment of pride and levity when someone yells out, "Who's that crazy naked mofo?"

**RULE NUMBER 5:** Paint your face. This is a must-do. When you walk out into the yard with a painted face you already have an edge. I like a simple "one side black, the other side white" look, but have fun! I've seen skulls, clowns, Jackson Pollock paintings, Egyptian symbols, brown paint that may or may not have been feces (see rule 8) and many more. If you can't do it yourself most prisons have a face-painting station for a cigarette or two.

**RULE NUMBER 6:** Play dead. It's not the strategy to use right out of the gate, mind you, but about midway through the riot there's no shame in curling up on the ground like you're dead. You might need to stab yourself to make it convincing but it's worth it. You get to watch all the pounding and kicking and sticking with sharp objects from a nice safe place. Again, afterward there's nothing funnier than one of the guys in the infirmary saying, "Ah shit, Burgundy, you wasn't dead!" and then having a good hearty laugh over it.

**RULE NUMBER 7:** Stay with your group! A prison is a population of men organized around different social groups. There are men who are uncomfortable around black people and other races. There are men who belong to various urban societies and motorbiking clubs. Each one of these groups can be very protective, so join! Be a joiner! I'm a loner, which is not the way to go in a riot, so I try to side with the homosexuals. These crafty she-hes know how to survive and thrive in a bloody riot. They are some devious tricky bastards and if you turn on them, out come the claws and the metal shivs and other stuff they hide up their butts.

**RULE NUMBER 8:** Have poop ready. Save up bags of your own poop and be prepared to throw it everywhere. No one likes to be hit with poop. Make sure you have lots of it too. The closer it can be to diarrhea but still be held in your hands, the better off you are. It's just basic human nature, going back to when we were monkeys. All animals, except dogs, try to avoid getting hit by poop. Aim for the face. It's magical stuff in a riot.

**RULE NUMBER 9:** Try reasoning. If you're cornered by a few thugs who want to stomp you to death, now's the time to try to reason with them. Every man carries within him a sense of fair play. We all have it, be it from our fathers, our ball-playing days or just spending time out in the world with other men in daily combat. You can count on this one basic truth. All men will see the logic in your argument and give way to a more peaceful, alternative solution. I am clearly messing with your head. (Something you learn to do in prison.) Prison riots are the very definition of unreasoned mayhem. You need to be on your toes at all times and trust no one.

**RULE NUMBER 10:** Be prepared for a life sentence. It doesn't matter if you've killed a man or if you're only doing a ninety-day stretch for forgery; you have to go into the riot believing you will never leave jail and like it. If you're dreaming of the day you leave, your opponent might smell hope on you. *Hope* is just another word for fear. Destroy all hope and turn yourself into a killing machine.

**RULE NUMBER 11:** Masturbate. Never tried this one but I saw it once in a Colombian prison, and let me tell you, everyone just left the guy alone. It's a bold move—not my style, but effective.

**RULE NUMBER 12:** Have fun. This might be the most important rule but so many people seem to forget it. It's a prison riot; have fun! Make a game of it. Sing to yourself. I sing songs from the musical *Hair.* Get punched and punch other people and smile. Don't forget to smile.

# MY NEIGHBOR RICHARD WELLSPAR

Last night around dinnertime I took a bag of dog crap that Baxter and I had conspired to save and set it on Richard Wellspar's front doorstep. I lit it on fire, rang his doorbell and ran away. Sweet revenge! I hurried back in the house and got to the window just in time to see Wellspar stomping out the fire on his stoop! What an idiot! It worked perfectly. Baxter was ecstatic! I said very loudly to Baxter, "That'll teach him to borrow something of mine and not return it." So about five minutes later, Richard comes to my door with the charred bag of poop.

"What is the meaning of this, Burgundy?" He's obviously very angry.

"I don't know what you're talking about, Richard. Is something the matter? I've been working on this airplane model for the last two hours." He didn't expect that, I'm sure. That was my strategic mind at work! I had gone to the hobby shop that morning and purchased a Grumman Bearcat World War II fighter plane model and put about half of it together. It actually was starting to look pretty good with the two wing pieces attached but I left it half-done and when I appeared at the front door holding the half-finished model it looked like I was in the middle of something that demanded great concentration and time. How could I have been involved in the flaming bag of poop? I was busy making my model.

"I heard you yell out your own name!" he barked. (It's true; I do sometimes yell my own name when I'm running and when I'm overly excited.) "Half the neighborhood saw you running from my house. What is wrong with you?"

"I'm a respected News Anchor," I said to buy some time while I thought of a better response. "Here's the situation, Richard, I am afraid of fire . . . so when I saw the burning bag of poop on your doorstep I rang your doorbell to warn you and then ran away in fear. You see, my daughter . . . Richardessa"—I came up with that fast!—"whose name is sort of like yours when you think about it—you two would have really hit it off—she died in a terrible awful fire about a week ago."

"Stop it, Burgundy. I don't like what you are doing and I want you to stop it. It's not funny."

"I wish I knew what you were talking about, Richard. We are neighbors and good friends. We say hello in the morning and borrow stuff from each other and return stuff. We're neighbors."

"You're not being a good neighbor, Burgundy. Just stop it." And he walked away. The leaf blower? Didn't even come up. So now I have determined that he means to steal my leaf blower. I am furious. It's time to put this little feud that he started into overdrive.

# FROM HUNTING TO PROTECTING: BURGUNDY AND THE ANIMAL KINGDOM AND THE DAWN OF THE JACKALOPES

I went jackalope hunting with Peter Lawford and Bobby Kennedy. I was in beautiful Las Vegas, where the women are loose and the slots are tighter than a librarian's vagina. Pardon my French! Anyway, I had an opportunity to meet both gentlemen when they took a fancy to the lady I was escorting. I was invited up to Lawford's private penthouse suite, where the three of us traded stories and sang show tunes all night long. Bobby was an excellent piano player before we lost him that blackest of days in California. I shall miss him dearly! He was a good man, ethical to the core—not like some of these politicians you see today. All of the Kennedys were made of the highest blue-blooded moral fiber and Bobby was no exception. Anyway we passed around three or four women between us, rotating and changing our styles, and then decided it was time for breakfast. They have the most sumptuous and amazing breakfast buffets in Vegas. If you've never been to one you are simply an idiot, an idiot to your friends and family and an idiot in the eyes of God. If there was a higher form of idiot, like a circus idiot's illegitimate child with an idiot donkey, then that would be you. Here's why: They have meat like you've never seen before! Three or four different types of bacon. They have Canadian bacon. They have regular or hickory bacon and thick-cut bacon. They have ham. They have steak. They have pork. Don't get me going on the merits of a Vegas buffet. Seriously! Get this, there's usually an omelet station and you can choose your own ingredients, be it ham or bacon or beans or cheese or all of it. The breaded material is limitless. Crescent rolls from France, sweet breads and doughnuts. Oh, and pancakes! Big fluffy, buttery pancakes like you've never tasted before. There are some fruit cups, for women I guess, but not really necessary. Two kinds of sausage, flat patties and wiener shaped. Holy Moses, I forgot the best part. When you are done scarfing all this down you simply hand the waiter your dirty plate and go back and get another clean plate for another round, free of charge! You heard me. It's all-you-can-eat! I would not lie about this. I know what you're saying: "Ron, some of the stories you tell in this novel are unbelievable." This buffet story is absolutely true. It's not the main gist of the whole story. It's really a story about hunting jackalopes with Bobby Kennedy and Peter Lawford, but I wasn't going to tell the story without the buffet part.

So there we were eating breakfast from the buffet when Kennedy starts talking about the legendary and elusive jackalope. A jackalope is a stronger and faster jackrabbit with antelope horns. They are believed to exist only in folktales and postcard shops throughout the Southwest. Anyway, Kennedy is going on and on about jackalopes when—wait one second, I forgot something about the buffet. The pancakes, I did them a real disservice. Yes they are fluffy and buttery, but they've also got different flavored fruit syrups you can pour over them, strawberry, blueberry, peach, whatever! AND— and this is big—whipped cream. So these pancakes are more like dessert than breakfast food. Just thought I should mention that. Also free refills on the coffee!

So Kennedy is going on about the jackalope when Lawford shouts out, "Let's go jackalope hunting!" Next thing I know I'm in a convertible Mercury Monterey rolling outside of Vegas in the high desert with Peter Lawford and Bobby Kennedy. Each one of us holds a service revolver handed to us by Kennedy's security team. Lawford swears that the only way to hunt jackalope is with handguns. I know what you're thinking: Ron Burgundy is a friend to animals; he wouldn't want to hunt them. Very true, I am, indeed, a great friend to all the Animal Kingdom, but I wasn't always. In fact there was a time when I just loved to hunt. You heard it here! Ron Burgundy, nature lover, hunted and killed animals for sport. Crossbows, rifles, knives, snares, traps, throwing stars, slingshots, dynamite, my bare hands and of course guns—I used them all. My lust for the blood sport was only outpaced by my lust for lovemaking.

Some weekends the whole news team would pack up the camping equipment and head up into the mountains for a few days of relaxing and hunting. I would bring the chow. Brian Fantana would bring various scents he said were useful for attracting "prey." It was usually just an assortment of his various colognes but they were also highly effective in attracting animals. I would say many of his colognes were better at attracting animals than women! Bears especially liked Night Stalker.

Funny story: One night we were all out on the town having a few drinks, seeing what we could stir up, when Fantana walks in drenched in Night Stalker. It's a heavy scent. Not all women go for it. It smells like cat box and old meat. This is downtown San Diego, mind you. Anyway Brian hits the dance floor, where he can show his moves to the ladies. Suddenly everyone is screaming and running for the doors. It's a bear, not a grizzly but a pretty big black bear. It probably traveled a hundred or two hundred miles to get to what it was smelling, Night Stalker. Poor guy quickly became disoriented and angry in the dance club. Bears are not cool with disco lights and Donna Summer. That's a bear fact not everyone knows. Suffice it to say it was a real mess! After that, San Diego made it illegal to have Night Stalker within the city limits.

Anyway, back to our hunting trips. Brick Tamland would usually pack a lunch box full of yarn or secret notes, and

Champ Kind, who to this day enjoys shooting and killing animals of any sort, would bring about forty to fifty guns of all sizes and makes. Too many guns really. (We once got pulled over by a state trooper in Nevada because Brian was driving 130 miles an hour through downtown Reno. The trooper asked to search the camper and was surprised by—and I think maybe a little scared of—what he found. None of the hundred or so guns we had in the camper or the trailer were registered. More than a few of them had been used in violent crimes and were sought after by prosecutors throughout the Southwest. There were even some grenades back in the trailer and a Russian-made rocket launcher. Luckily it was Nevada. We got out of there with a slap on the wrist and a twenty-dollar fine. That particular trip turned out to be a huge disaster, which is an entirely different story! Let's just say there's a big difference between hunting and insurrection.)

Mainly our little hunting excursions didn't amount to much more than four drunk guys in the woods shooting off guns and eating cans of soup! I don't even remember bagging many animals when the news team got together to hunt. It wasn't about that. It was more about friends yelling and not shaving. However I do recall one time when we probably killed a mountain lion, or maybe more than one. I say that because we spent a night in Montana fighting off mountain lions. Once again Brian had one of his colognes with him, I think it was something he called Erotic Dawn. Whatever it was, it sure attracted mountain lions. I don't care what naturalists say, mountain lions are not solitary creatures. They can organize and work in groups if the need arises. They can even work with other animals, like raccoons and hawks, if they want something bad enough. They wanted Erotic Dawn real bad. We spent that night completely sober shooting semiautomatic weapons out into the dark, just praying we were hitting the lions. Scary stuff. Fond memories. I can now look back on those days and laugh! I'm a different man today and soon enough you'll see why. My transformation happened almost all at once at a point in my life I still call "the Dawn of the Jackalope."

So back to the jackalope tale. Me, Kennedy and Lawford are driving in the desert. There's plenty of booze in the car—this was back in the days when you could legally drive drunk. Most men in the late sixties who were responsible and held down respectable nine-to-five jobs drove home drunk every night. No one said anything then! I don't know. Times change. Frankly it would not have mattered if we were swerving all over the highway, because we were definitely off the main roads in the middle of nowhere. At one point I remember asking Lawford if he knew where we were going and he said, "To hell!" Kennedy just laughed and shot his pistol into the air. After about five or six hours of driving through the desert we came to a spot where we parked the car. Lawford got very quiet. He whispered, "We are in the land of the jackalope. Keep all of your senses alive." We got out to walk. We carried whatever bottles of beer and bourbon we could find in the car along with some flares and boxes of ammo, then headed out on foot. We walked for hours, only stopping to drink the bourbon. The heat was punishing. The sole force pushing us on under the brutal sun and over uneven desert terrain was the chance encounter with the vicious and fast-attacking jackalope.

I'll tell you this. If you want to get to know a man, I mean really get to know him, go jackalope hunting with him. We three got very close out there as we slowly started to die from heatstroke and dehydration. Bobby confided in me that he was responsible for Marilyn Monroe's death. He had been in love with her long before his brother John but if he couldn't have her, then no one could. He forced pills on her and left her to die. Peter told me he once had a three-way with Frank Sinatra and his daughter Nancy.

There's a chance none of this was true of course. Men say strange things before they are about to die of heatstroke. Our brains were like hot cream of barley soup. I confessed to both of them that I stole dinosaur bones from the Museum of Natural History in New York City. (That actually was true. I did steal those bones, but I needed them.) We wandered aimlessly for days. When the beer and bourbon ran out we experienced a new kind of torture. Bobby Kennedy would not shut up. He was a bit of a Boy Scout and a know-it-all. He was arrogant, like every Kennedy. The kind of arrogance you admire and appreciate and look up to until you have to listen to it all day. Lawford and I quickly grew to hate him and his endlessly blathering mouth. Unfortunately we also knew he was our best chance at survival. He found us water underneath the sand and sustenance in lizards, snakes and cacti. He was an excellent marksman with a revolver as well. Crossing him might have cost us our lives, so we toed the line and nodded our heads when he talked. The sun came up maybe six or seven times on us while we were out there. Buzzards began circling on day five. Meanwhile we hadn't seen one jackalope. Lawford was beginning to scare me with his Captain Ahab–like declarations. "Gentlemen, there's jackalopes afoot." Or "I smell jackalope." I was beginning to think maybe the jackalope was some sort of hoax made up for tourists!

Without upsetting Peter Lawford I walked Kennedy out into the desert where we could talk alone. We sat on a rock under the moonlight while Lawford painted his own blood on his face. I quietly spoke to Bobby of my doubts. He confessed to me he hated politics and that he really wanted to be a maintenance man in a luxury hotel but that his father, Joseph, was a real asshole. I tried to stay on point with my concern about the existence of jackalopes and whether we needed to be out in the desert at all. He confided in me that Jackie O was a better lay than Marilyn and that the woman had a mouth on her that could suck the chrome off a trailer hitch. I wanted to listen to his concerns and confidences but I really felt we needed to form a majority opinion so we could talk Lawford into heading back toward civilization. He understood, I think, but wanted me to know that his brother Ted was gay and couldn't handle it and so he drank. I took this in—that was a big one—but I straight-up asked him if he thought jackalopes were real! He didn't answer for a long time. I could hear coyotes howling off in the distance. They would be getting close soon. Somewhere a desert owl announced his loneliness with a mournful hoot. The desert is a cold mistress. Finally, Bobby sat up and said these words to me from the poet Aeschylus: "Wisdom comes alone through suffering." He then walked out into the darkness. I didn't see him again. Like everyone I was shocked and saddened by his death. I had the solemn duty of having to report it on the evening news. I ended the night's broadcast with another Aeschylus quotation that maybe Bobby would have appreciated: "Call no man happy until he is dead." When I awoke the next morning Peter Lawford was standing over me holding a pistol to my face. "Where's Kennedy?" he yelled. I told him that he'd walked off into the night but he was having none of it. He was sure I had eaten him. Lawford had smeared a clown's smile on his face and three lines across his forehead. He also had blisters all over his head from the sun. He was nude. I tried to reason with him. I told him how much I liked Bobby and that I would never eat him. Peter was not convinced. He told me he was going to have to kill me to see if he could get his friend Bobby out of my belly. This was nonsense, I thought, but he cocked the gun aimed at my face. Now, here's where the story gets kind of unbelievable, but it's absolutely true, as is every word of this novel. As I was about to get shot by Peter Lawford, a voice so smooth and soothing came from the wind and spoke these words: "Kill not this man!" Lawford and I were stunned. Who spoke? Peter started spinning and shooting into the air. It was no use. There was no one there. Both of us were trembling in fear . . . but then we saw it: a jackalope! And then another, and soon we were surrounded. Thousands of jackalopes, squealing and thumping. It was unbearable. Then after several minutes the squealing and thumping stopped. The biggest jackalope of all approached us and spoke. "My name is Sekannawan, son of Kokatah, cousin to the wind, king of the jackalopes. This violence you wish on each other cannot happen on our sacred ground. You, the one called Ron Burgundy"—he looked at me—"why does this man wish to bring you into eternal darkness?"

"This man," I said to the jackalope, "believes I have eaten Senator Bobby Kennedy. He believes Mr. Kennedy is alive and in my belly."

"Is this true, Peter Lawford?" asked Sekannawan.

"Yes, proud mythical beast. I believe the senator has been eaten by this man."

"Not so," said the jackalope king. "Bobby Kennedy was given permission to walk free from here and with our aid he made it back to civilization. He is enjoying the breakfast buffet at the Desert Inn even as I speak."

Well, you can imagine how this really burned my britches. Suddenly I didn't care a lick about this talking jackalope king and I let him know it. "Now, you listen to me! My name is Ron Burgundy and I'm not going to sit here listening to any half rabbit, half antelope blabber on while Bobby Kennedy is enjoying a delicious breakfast buffet. I WILL NOT STAND FOR IT!"

"Then you have no choice but to enter the Ring of Lost Horns and fight me unto the death!" said Sekannawan the jackalope king.

"Then I shall fight you!" I cried.

"Be careful, Burgundy." Peter was back on my side. "He will tear your limbs off and eat your liver while you are still alive. He will feed your eyes to his children while you can still feel the pain. The raw sound of gnashing baby jackalope teeth on your eyes will drive you to insanity before you die!" It was truly the most emotive I had seen Peter Lawford since his turn as Theodore Laurence in *Little Women*. I told him as much and he was grateful for the notice.

We were paraded some miles to a circular patch in the desert. The ground was littered with the horns of dead jackalopes. It was a gruesome sight to be sure but my mind was focused on that buffet. I couldn't stop thinking about maybe one day possibly wrapping two pancakes around a western omelet in the shape of a huge spongy burrito. I would call it "the Breakfast Burgito" and it would be enjoyed the world over. In my reverie I hardly heard the sounding of the jackalope yell signaling the beginning of the fight. Sekannawan came at me fast. His little jackrabbit feet exploded his muscular body off the ground. His antlers pointed right at my face as he flew through the air. It was like a grenade had gone off and the shrapnel was coming at me. I had time for one move and one move only. My two hands went instinctively to guard my face. The antlers hit my hands with surprisingly little force. He was a lightweight. I grabbed ahold of both antlers and tore him in half. The fight was over. A thousand jackalopes stood in mute silence, stunned by the death of their king. But soon the silence grew to a murmur and then a growl. "Kill him!" they yelled! And just like that they were on us, Lawford and me. Ripping and gnashing and tearing, they tried their best, but we were killing jackalopes faster than you can say *omelet fixins*.

"ENOUGH!" came the cry of a female jackalope. Suddenly they all stopped attacking. When she spoke I knew that she was their queen. "My name is Kokenta, queen of the jack-alopes. I say free this man! He has honored the law of the Ring of Lost Horns. He is worthy of our respect and admiration and shall hereafter be known as Ron Burgundy, king of the jackalopes." I think she was trying to save face, because clearly Lawford and I were going to rip up their entire population in about ten minutes.

"Great queen," I said, "I do not wish to be worshipped as your king but only to return to the Desert Inn for their breakfast buffet."

"You can return, Ron Burgundy, under one condition," she spoke.

"Name your price, wise jackalope queen."

"From this day forth you shall harm not beasts of the wild for any reason other than survival of thyself."

I was slow to answer but when the words finally came I felt a great relief, like a magical feeling of being one with the universe had overtaken me and I was suddenly free. I answered her demand thusly: "I will indeed honor your condition and from this day forth, this dawn of the jackalopes, I, Ron Burgundy, son of Claude Burgundy, will harm not any beasts of the wild unless my own life is challenged."

"Go in peace, Ron Burgundy," my new friend Kokenta said. "Your name will forever be sung in our epic songs. Your deeds will not be forgotten by the jackalopes! Make haste. The breakfast buffet ends at eleven thirty." And off the thousand jackalopes went, racing into the desert. I have not seen one since. But, yes, they have seen me.

My experience with the jackalopes was deep and life alter-
ing. I began a journey of new understanding in relation to
the Animal Kingdom as a whole. Baxter, my very best friend
and dog, was my constant companion and guide through this
new consciousness. I am a sensitive man unafraid to express
my feelings. I have been known to cry from time to time. I've
never made it through the movie *One on One* with Robby Ben-
son because I get too choked up. It's so very emotional. If
you haven't seen it, do so, it's a real treat. A young college
basketball player with great one-on-one skills is forced to play
in a system of offense and defense that severely constricts his
style. It's torturous to watch. The overbearing coach, played
by G. D. Spradlin, simply won't let the kid create on the court.
Whatever you do, don't tell me how it ends. I have never seen
the ending and I doubt I ever will. The waterworks start
flowing as soon as I hear the Seals and Crofts song "My Fair
Share" and because of my loud sobbing, almost screaming really, I am always asked to leave the theater. Annette O'Toole
plays a bitchy but softhearted tutor—Oh boy . . . I'm having
a hard time getting through this right now! Forget I brought
up the movie *One on One*. It's just too damn emotional for me
to even write about it.

My point here is simple. I am a sensitive man. I'm not
afraid to pick a flower or delight in a butterfly or go for a skip.
I care about the world around me and all of its creatures. Now
when I see a manatee or a dingo or a hyena or a toucan or a
giraffe or a leopard or a tortoise or a cow or a baboon or a

Gila monster, I have no desire to kill it. Take the wild baboon for an example. If you run at a baboon with your arms waving, yelling with your shirt off, which I have done, the animal will see it as an act of aggression and run full speed right at you. His only thought will be how to get at your face and tear it off so he can eat your head meat. I don't speak baboon. I confess I don't speak any animal language. However, Baxter can communicate with almost all of God's creatures and I can converse with him. On that particular safari when I ran out to a baboon to play a joke on him I was nearly torn to shreds. He was feet away from chewing off my whole face when Baxter barked out, "No, proud race of ape! He is your brother!" To which the baboon responded, "This thing is no ape!"

Baxter would have none of it and he said to the baboon, "He is an upright ape, no more dignified than you, great baboon, but simply one that can drive a car and uses small sharp knives to cut the hair on his face."

"Why is he running at me?"

"The human man is not smart. He does not understand basic body language."

"He could have gotten killed," the baboon warned. (All of this conversation was related to me later by Baxter on the plane ride home.)

"I have had to save him many times from all sorts of animals in the Animal Kingdom," said Baxter.

"I don't understand, what's in it for you?"

"He puts dry dog food in a bowl for me."

"A devil's bargain!"

"He is my friend. I sleep with him when he has not 'scored.' I sleep with him often."

"What is your name?"

"My name is Baxter and his name is Ron Burgundy."

"Well, Baxter, you tell your friend Ron Burgundy not to run at baboons the way he did. It's weird."

"I shall relate that to him. You are a gentle soul."

"And you are a wise dog. Go now. I am hungry and I will want to eat either you or the Ron Burgundy."

"We will take our leave. Can I smell your red butt?"

"Of course."

An animal that understands that you respect him, from the fearsome white shark to the impulsive and grumpy bear, will be more willing to treat you with respect.

Over time I have come to understand the Animal Kingdom as one great hierarchy. The noble eagle sits at the top. He is God's greatest creation, soaring through the skies with magnificent splendor and grace! His watchful eye looks over us all. I am in awe of the eagle and I believe one day when the skies fall and great chasms of doom open up to swallow mankind, it will be the eagle that rescues and guides those of us worthy (that would be me and my news team for sure) into the next land. I have several wood carvings of eagles in my home for this reason. One of them has a removable head and a hollowed-out body where you can hide some keys or half pencils like the kind you get at a golf course. If the noble eagle is at the top of the Animal Kingdom, then surely the lowly sea otter is at the bottom. They are the dumbest, most stupid animals out there. I can't even imagine what kind of hell we would be in for if the sea otter ever took control of the world. Simply put, they would ruin it. I don't hate them but I sure wouldn't trust them with maintaining order. Baxter confided in me once that talking to sea otters was like talking to aerobics instructors. I don't doubt it. They are self-centered and boring and all they want to talk about is fish. Meanwhile Baxter tells me that most eagles think like ancient Greeks with minds sharper than Socrates'. Baxter has also told me on several occasions that eagles intimidate him. His small dog brain is no match for the cerebral majesty of the eagle.

As a kind of sidebar I would like to say wild eagles do not make great pets. I was offered a wild eagle by a Russian I had come to know through the world of high-stakes archery. We both had an interest in falconry. (I have owned several world-class falcons over the years.) This man—I will call him "Glavtec" because he would definitely not want me to reveal his true identity—had six bald eagles in the trunk of his car that he was trying to unload. He was in to me for a lot of archery money. I REALLY wanted one of those eagles but I knew it was illegal to own a bald eagle in this country. I decided if I kept the eagle inside my house no one would be the wiser and I could have my cake and eat it too. I threw the eagle in a pillowcase and took him home. Well, day one the eagle tore up everything in my house. Day two he scratched up Baxter and me pretty badly. Day three he got caught in a fan and while trying to rescue him I got scratched up worse than before. Day four he sat on the couch almost lifeless, watching TV and possibly contemplating suicide. Day five he began working on a strategy for escape. Day six he was polite and even ate dinner with us at the table. Day seven he allowed me to place a small Uncle Sam hat on his head and posed for a picture with me and Baxter in our red, white and blue swimsuits. Day eight I taught him to drive a miniature fire truck in a comical way and he looked like he was enjoying himself. On the ninth day Baxter and I decided to take our new best friend for a walk on the beach. The minute I opened the door he flew away. He had been planning it all along! He was just playing with me to get free. Ingenious! He still, to this day, attacks me when he sees me. I'm forever watching the skies. He truly is a magnificent bird.

Where does man fit in this great chain of being? I'll tell you. Right between the narwhal and the puma, and that's pretty close to the top, my friend. I would say humans are positioned maybe a hundred or so animals from the top. Pretty good considering there are more than a thousand animals. Things like cheetahs, hermit crabs and salmon are definitely higher than us, but then donkeys, parrots and daddy longlegs are below us. It really puts things in perspective when you come to understand the science of the Animal Kingdom and where we as humans stand within it, or Human Positionology, as it is known in science circles. I try not to lord it over the dumber lower animals, like horses and woodpeckers, because I always know there are more intelligent animals, like the squirrel and fruit bats, that can look down on me! Through my experiences with the jackalopes and my understanding of the great chain of being I have become a friend to all nature. I no longer hunt for pleasure. I don't condemn those who do.

The Socratic Eagle

Rooster

Hermit Crab

Salmon

Cheetah

Fruit Bat

Squirrel

Puma

Man

Narwhal

Dog

Cat

Donkey

Parrot

Daddy Longlegs

The Lowly Sea Otter

**CHART OF HUMAN POSITIONOLOGY**

Champ Kind, my friend and an award-winning sports jour-nalist, kills, on average, around five to six hundred animals a year. He loves to hunt. He would hunt caged chickens if it were legal. Maybe he does anyway! I know every year he goes off on his annual hunting trip to some secret island with a group of men known only as the Dark Watch. I don't know what they hunt. I don't want to know. I say live and let live, which might not be what they say at all. Funny situations.

Finally, I want to say a word about cats. They are wonderful!

# ABOUT WOMEN

Over the years I've had an ever-evolving understanding of the female sex. I credit Veronica Corningstone, my wife, my lover and my sex partner, as the lady who changed my views on women. Before I met Veronica I had some anti-quated ideas of how women should conduct themselves in the world. For the longest time I didn't like seeing a woman in the workplace unless she was getting me coffee or bending over or both. Often I would put a cup of coffee on the floor and ask a woman to get it for me. I know it sounds crazy but I wasn't sure women could read. When I saw them typing I just assumed they were copying shapes or making noise for no reason. I didn't know if women knew how to count money. I thought women had underdeveloped brains like the brains of softheaded people. Then there was the whole idea of menstruation. It made no sense to me and science didn't seem to have any answers. How could a person dying of blood loss be allowed to work in a man's office? Frankly I'm still having problems with this one. The science just isn't there yet. We need greater study in this area but I'm willing to concede women should be allowed in the workplace alongside men. I can laugh at some of the naive things I used to think, but much of it you could write off because of the times. The times were different. Before 1970 women were here on this earth to cook food and give men boners. You certainly couldn't associate them with delivering the news. There was the whole credibility problem. I wasn't alone in believing that women could not be trusted. I once bet Edward R. Murrow that a dog would anchor the news before a woman, and I believed it. Women were considered nothing more than sex objects. They were valued more for their legs, their butts and their tits than for anything else. Times sure have changed! Heck, now in television news and I guess just about everywhere else women are respected for their brains. Appearance means very little! Go figure! When I see a woman walking down the street in high heels and a short skirt I no longer drool like a hungry zombie. I think to myself, "Hmmmm, I wonder what kind of brain that foxy mama has?" Veronica did that to me. She's got brains, all right, and I married her for that reason. Of course Veronica also just happens to have a grade-A dumper and some first-class tits.

For many years I was asked to attend sensitivity training. I got hit with sexual misconduct suits left and right, at least twenty a year for a while. My hands were always leaving me and going places. I stood too close to women. I used words like *boobies* and *knockers* and *jugs* and *jigglers* and *melons* to compliment my coworkers. At one point I was told by my lawyer that it was safer if I never talked to women. But of course that is ridiculous. My old-fashioned transgressions aside, I do know a lot about the ladies. Without being modest, I've found that women cannot keep their hands off me. It's true. I've slept with more women than six Wilt Chamberlains. I've made love to women in the same room—heck, in the same bed—with Wilt. Wilt and I have—oh no I won't; that's a story for a different kind of book. Besides, the young women we were with that night, Tracy Karns and Debra Sanlinger, may not want me to tell that story. It's pretty dirty.

Suffice it to say I've learned quite a lot about the fairer sex over the years just through experience alone. If you add to that my extensive reading in scientific journals and my interviews with great lovemakers like myself and Geraldo Rivera, you could say that I'm probably the world's greatest authority on the subject of women. I could write a whole book just about women. Someday I will, believe me. It would have a bunch of pictures—not just nude women either. They would be on horseback or in cocktail outfits or wearing cheerleading dresses. I would show them in natural settings like offices and beaches, or maybe even on the farm. Each woman in the book would talk about her favorite things, like what turns her on and what her measurements are, stuff like that. Then I would have pictures of these women in their underwear, probably just so you could see a little bit more. After a few photos of the women in their clothes I would then have nude photos of them. Maybe one part of this book I'm thinking about could have a special unfolding-page section in the middle that gives you a big picture of one of the women completely naked. I don't know! The book is not fully formed in my mind just yet. Perhaps if I had chapters about stereo equipment and new suit styles it would be helpful for men too. I bet a guy could put a book like this out every couple of months! I would sure read it. My point is I know an awful lot about women.

Women on the whole tend to be more emotional than men. I may be the rare exception. I'm more better at emotional stuff than women. I'm actually more better than women at a lot of stuff. I can balance a basketball on my finger for more than twenty seconds. I bet I can run faster than most women. Cheetahs are the fastest mammals on earth. I know how to spell *Mississippi* backward—what am I doing? This isn't a contest. Anyway, women turn on the waterworks for just about any reason but mostly for manipulation. No one likes to see a woman cry and women know it. They use the crying thing all the time to get what they want. It starts when they are babies and doesn't stop until the dirt is shoveled over them. For whatever reason men stop using tears at around seven years old and start using their brains instead to control their surroundings. In scientific terms women's cranial development is said to be retarded but their powers of manipulation are far in advance of most men's by the time they are five years old. This is basic developmental stuff, by the way, and you could read it in any journal of human development. There's a special "manipulation gene" in women that has been discovered or will be discovered. This gene, which surely exists, controls the crying and lying sections of the frontal cortex lobular section of the brain. It allows women to trick men into all kinds of situations.

A woman's sneaky and underhanded manipulation can take many forms and can be quite cunning and subtle. Here's a standard conversation I might have with my wife and glorious sexual partner, Veronica.

**Ron**
**I was thinking about going out with the boys tonight, maybe having a few drinks?**

**Veronica**
**Sounds fun.**

**Ron**
**Just me and the boys.**

**Veronica**
**You need to get out. You've been working very hard.**

Well, you can see how infuriating this kind of subtle manipulation can be! Every word is so well chosen to cause pain. It's like they control your mind! I once wore a motorcycle helmet with a dark shield on a date with a woman I thought was trying to control my mind. I was too afraid to take it off for fear she might try to change my plans using manipulative word combinations and crying. I literally could not hear or see her the whole date. In the end it worked out. We made sweet and long-lasting love but I stayed inside the helmet so as not to let her connect to me and my mind.

Of course, for most of the women in my life I didn't need a helmet to protect me from their controlling ways. I have an automatic shutoff switch inside my brain that lets me listen to a woman speak without hearing a word. For about a ten-year period, up until I was smitten with Veronica, I used the time that women spoke to me as a chance to think up songs or poems or make up new games. It was a valuable use of my time. A woman would come up to me and maybe start a sentence like "Ron, I need to speak to you. . . ." If she was serious I would nod and look concerned and say "Okay" and "Right away" every so often, but inside I was off thinking about something else, something fun. I made up the game Piddly-Woop while some woman was talking to me. It's a complicated but fun game for the whole family.

I'm not going to lie, I heard this a lot from women throughout the sixties: "Are you listening to me?" A lot. So to be honest I'm not sure I perfected my "shutoff switch" method. I know that my colleague Champ Kind has never listened to a woman talk for more than eight seconds. He shuts off and just smiles and waits for them to stop moving their mouths. If you asked him I don't think he could remember two sentences a woman has said to him. It's remarkable really. For him it's like they don't even exist as speaking animals.

Looking back on it, I think plenty of women thought maybe I was rude. It didn't really matter though. In those days there were so many women who wanted to make it with a number one News Anchor that it was just the law of averages. The way I figured it, if I batted one for twenty, that would make for a batting average of fifty. Those are Hall of Fame numbers, my friend, Hall of Fame.

As a Hall of Fame ladies' man (an institution I am lobbying to create, by the way), I don't think anyone in the world would mind if I gave up some of my secrets for how to meet, bed and marry the woman of your dreams.

# HOW TO MEET, BED AND MARRY THE WOMAN OF YOUR DREAMS

Courtship is as old as the earliest days of fire. Men have forever pursued females in poetry and song and with feats of daring. Little has changed from those early days of courtship. We gentlemen still recite poems and sing and try to outdo other men for the hearts of women. I often dream of the medieval days, when men wearing robes made of thick woven carpet lifted heavy goblets of wine and sang to their paramours. Even though the great banquets and royal feasts of olden days are long gone, I feel like I would have been right at home in their giant halls. I've often imagined myself

atop the turret of some noble castle on the Rhine with my fal-
con, Leander, perched on my arm. I think in a past life I was
maybe a baron or possibly an earl and that I had many lands
and great wealth and an eye patch. I was known throughout
the region as a generous landowner but ruthless when I had
to be. I could be quite swift with justice but I was never accused of being unfair. If you've seen my dining room in my
house, then you know it's a passion of mine to imagine such
things. I've commissioned murals on the walls of my dining
room with scenes of me throughout history. A local artist by
the name of Vincent St. Vincent-Pierre was paid handsomely,
perhaps too handsomely, to illustrate me in heroic situations
throughout time. While dining at the Burgundy house, guests
enjoy rich oil paintings of me as an explorer on a clipper ship
sailing for the New World. They can turn their heads and I'm
represented as a proud slave in the Roman Colosseum, having just vanquished a lion! St. Vincent-Pierre also portrayed
me as a noble savage who first lays eyes on Lewis and Clark
from a bluff high above the wide Missouri. Guests often com-
ment on the painting entitled *Justice for All,* where I am standing with my arm around my good friend Nat Turner in a field
of bloodied and hacked white slave owners. It's really quite
a room! On the ceiling, above the table, St. Vincent-Pierre
painted his masterpiece, Veronica and me making love in the
nude as a panoply of exotic animals look on in wonder. It's
the room I'm most proud of in my house. I suspect the room
will be carefully dismantled when I pass and donated to the
San Diego fine arts museum. Look at me! I was supposed to
be talking about courtship. There I go again. The problem

I'm discovering while writing this chronicle is that I'm just too darn interesting!

I don't have the facts in front of me but I'm pretty sure the ratio of women to men in this country is approximately one and one-quarter women to every eight males. It's a problem and we should really import more women into this country— not from England, Jesus Christ, NOT FROM ENGLAND. Some countries, like France I believe, have thirty women for every man, which accounts for why Frenchmen always have beautiful girlfriends and wives. If you put a Frenchman in a country where he had to fight it out with real men for the love of a woman, he would fail miserably and be left with only the dogs.

With such a low ratio of women in this country it makes it hard to meet and then court them. Hanging out at the ball game or the Elks Lodge is not going to do it. You could go where they go—the hair parlor, for instance, but you end up looking pretty stupid in a hair parlor. I've sat in women's hair parlors before. It's only a matter of time before you are asked to leave. The best places to meet women are places where both sexes mingle—churches, parks, department stores and supermarkets. There's a strategy for each location.

For instance, let's talk about supermarkets. Women like a man who is confident, and nothing says confidence more than beef. When I'm in a supermarket, whether it be to pick up a gallon of milk or to get some coffee, I take my cart straight for the meat department and pile it full of steaks. Make sure the cart is overflowing with steaks. Don't worry, you don't have to buy them. It's only for show—you can ditch the cart later in the bread aisle, but while you're in the supermarket, for two to three hours, you need to push around a cart weighted down with cuts of red meat . . . and NO CHICKEN. Maybe some pork, but make sure you have lots of sirloin and ribs. Women go nuts! They see all that beef and it triggers within them something from the cavemen days. They just start thinking of procreating. I promise you if you push around a shopping cart with two hundred pounds of meat cuts in a supermarket you will get respect from women. I like to throw in a few cans of beans and twenty or so packages of bacon to add some variety. A box of condoms is too suggestive and shows a real lack of class. No, the best course is to simply walk around the supermarket, humming along with the piped-in music, pushing your cart of meat in front of you like you don't have a care in the world. You can sometimes "accidentally" bump into a woman and then say something like "Sorry, it looks like my meat got away from me!" If the woman smiles, then follow her—by all means follow her. Some won't smile. The crabby ones will look at you like you're some kind of homeless man and recoil. They are not worth the effort. They're not real women anyway. They might even be lesbians. More than likely women who do not fall for the ole meat cart routine are lesbians.

In a department store you can't walk around with a cart full of meat. It's stupid, and frankly you look crazy because most department stores don't sell meat. The thing to do in a department store is to carry around eight or nine suits. Go straight to the suit department and get eight or nine suits and then start walking around the whole store. Purchasing power alone is a real turn-on for all women, but when they see suits they react like they've seen a shopping cart full of meat. You have the money to buy eight suits. You have the class to wear a suit. You are desirable. It's simple. Some guys will head over to the women's wear section, maybe grab a bra to hold, and start crying and talking about the "breakup." It's a good ruse. There are women who fall for it but ultimately you need to look secure, and bawling on the floor with underwear in your hand is not very secure looking. If you need to shout out, "I'm buying eight suits today," that's okay. Imagine being a woman (not putting on the clothes and walking around in front of a mirror; I mean just imagine it with your brain); now imagine you're in a store and you see some handsome man with a new toaster in his hand and you are intrigued, but then out of nowhere you hear a loud voice proclaim, "I'm buying eight suits!" And around a corner comes a man holding eight suits. I rest my case.

PTA meetings are real winners. It doesn't matter if you have a kid in the school. Walk in, sit down and wait. When people start popping up and talking, stand up and talk, maybe cry, but whatever you do make it passionate. I usually try something like "We need to address the issue of safe zones. I know it's controversial but I am for it!" I blabber on for a bit about keeping children safe and then I might wrap up my speech with something like ". . . and one more thing: I drive a Chrysler LeBaron." Women love that you care about children but it's even better when they hear you drive something like a LeBaron or a Stratus; they get wet down below. It also helps to have a step stool. You really want to tower over everyone else in the room. If some nosey body gets in your face and asks you what grade your child is in at the school, you need to run away. No harm no foul, just keep running until you are safely out of the neighborhood. If you're jumping fences, look out for the bigger dogs.

Fortunately for me meeting women has never been a real issue. I am a very big deal. I have been for some time. When you are the number one News Anchor in San Diego you are basically a rock star. When you make it to the network you are a god. Women just want what I have. They want to be close to it. They want to be a part of the magic. Brian Fantana, who does a lot of reporting from the street, literally has to fight the women off with a stick. He once confided in me he's never masturbated—not once—because it has always been easier for him to just go ahead and have sex with a woman. In fact he sometimes fantasizes about masturbation while having sex with women. That's what being in the news game is like. Just ask Brian Williams. That guy uses Velcro to keep his pants shut. He doesn't have time to keep buttoning and unbuttoning them with all the classy tail he gets. Being a News Anchor is so close to being a god on so many levels that you start to think like one. You start to believe it's your right to descend on women and impregnate them with demigod babies. Those were simpler times, of course, when gods could just come down and have sex with any mortal they wanted. I would give my right nut to live in those days with the gods, but no such luck; I got stuck in this age of horseshit. Anyway, I digress. Once you've got the woman interested it's time to think about stage two: How am I going to get this woman in the sack?

Here again it helps to be a number one News Anchor. Women just want to jump in bed with me. I can't help it; it's just something I live with. Every once in a while a woman comes along who does not want to sleep with me. It's weird but it happens. My first reaction is always the same: Do I look like the man who killed her dog? If it's not that, then I know she's just a psychologically damaged frigid woman who needs a little Burgundy thaw. I start by asking her out on a date. Now is not the time to be cheap. Take her to an Olive Garden or a Red Lobster. If you have a skill, like playing the flute, or you can juggle, now is the time to spring it on her. The mystery you have inside you unfolds. She's probably thinking, if you can juggle, what else can you do? She's going to be intrigued. I sometimes will hit a woman with my amazing knowledge of dinosaurs. I might tell her that birds are considered a subgroup of dinosaurs by many paleontologists or that the word *dinosaur* means "terrible lizard." Women can't believe what they are hearing. They see how smart you are and then you tell them it's just the tip of the iceberg! This is also a great time to blow hot air her way. Women respond well to humid, pungent hot air (see chapter on effective breath).

Get them talking. Women love to talk. You don't have to listen, as mentioned before, but you do have to let them talk, and believe me, they will yammer on like howler monkeys. Pretend you are interested if you can. It's not a deal breaker if you can't, mind you, but it helps. Most women understand that you are not interested. Scientists have proven that by the time a woman is in her late teens she knows that men will not pay any attention to the noises coming out of her mouth.

That's not to say women have nothing to say. Please, don't misinterpret me. The last thing I need is a bunch of angry feminists picketing my house and throwing pies at me. I know what that feels like and I don't like it. You would think I would like it! Pies are delicious, but pies can also be hurtful. There have been some great women talkers over the years. I could list so many! Smart women have made their mark on history and I know the names of many if not all of them. (NOTE: Find list of smart women for later draft.) Anyway women love to talk and if you can manage some fake interest it's a great way to get them comfortable.

Once she is comfortable it's time to be direct. Nothing works quite like leaving a lady in a room for a few minutes and then returning wearing only your best Nordstrom or Crabtree and Evelyn bathrobe. Talk about a winning strategy! Women will react in different ways but believe me, you will always get a reaction! Leave the bathrobe open for a hint of what awaits within. A glimpse or suggestion of chest hair, maybe a little belly, can send a girl to the moon, wild with anticipation—not all women, mind you, but a select few. Keep in mind these time-tested strategies are all from before I married my best friend and sexually adventurous wife, Veronica. The bathrobe ploy, as I called it, was used many times to great success in the home or outside just walking around. I sometimes wore the open bathrobe through the supermarket or at work. I think now there are laws that prohibit open bathrobe wearing in places of business. I don't know, it's hard to keep up with all the laws people make. Sometimes I think people who can't build stuff or report the news or do anything useful spend their time making up laws. The world would be a better place if men and women could walk around in open bathrobes.

Once you are in the sack there's very little I need to tell you that you can't find out on your own. I was lucky to have Jenny Haggleworth, sixteen years my senior, for my first go-round. She knew what she was doing all right! For most young men learning to make love I recommend cruising retirement villages to see if they can scrounge up some old tail. Women in their seventies and eighties make great guides through the complicated world of the sensual arts. A young man of twenty can really benefit from a few days in the sack with an old prune or a French whore. Of course, where are you going to find a French whore in times of peace, huh? Anyway after a night d'amour you can usually sneak away unharmed. Unless you have fallen in love. If that's the case you might have to start thinking about marriage.

The Holy Bible teaches us that marriage was invented by Helen of Troy to keep men from ruling over Canaan. It's in Deuteronomy somewhere, I believe. The exact quote is, "So sayeth Helen of Troy that unto her Joseph shall be husband to the woman soeth he hath not manly poweres hence forth and the woman shall have dominion over the domain." Something like that. I'm paraphrasing I think, or I made it up. It doesn't matter. Most historians believe the King James Bible was written by Shakespeare anyway, and we all know what kind of ladies' man he was. The real point I'm making here is you need to go into marriage lightly, my friend. The two sexes were never meant to live together and that's just a fact.

I don't have the numbers in front of me but I believe that all marriages in this country end in divorce. I can't for the life of me think of a marriage that hasn't ended in divorce. There must be one. It would be interesting to find that couple and ask them what went wrong. Why did they stay together when they obviously needed to get away from each other? Are they lying? Are they secretly divorced but they just wanted to be on the news? How could they look each other in the face for so long? This is all hypothetical of course. We don't even know if such a couple exists. Go ahead, get married, I don't care. Get married over and over again. It's very American and for that reason I am for it.

## MY NEIGHBOR: THE PLOT THICKENS

My neighbor, the one who borrowed my leaf blower and didn't return it, is dating an old broad that I slept with thirty years ago. Cynthia Spaller is her name and honestly she's still got it. I want to shake the hands of the plastic surgeon who kept those two boulders up in the air. Frankly she's too good for him. Anyway he's throwing a block party and he didn't invite me. How do you not invite Ron Burgundy? I'm a living legend. Okay, Wellspar, let's see where this goes.

# MY HISTORY OF MEXICO

I decided to do it. I'm going to write a history of Mexico. Someone's gotta do it! I figure it's my gift to the Mexican peoples. I'm passionate about history and I'm not sure we want to leave it up to Mexicans. I brought it up in an earlier chapter and I just couldn't let the idea go. This is just the first chapter and the book is in no way designed like I would like it. As I said before it will definitely be bound in rich Corinthian leather, about two feet by three feet in size and about eight inches thick. It will have many fine illustrations and smell like a new pair of cowboy boots. So without further ado . . . here is the first chapter of my long-awaited history of Mexico.

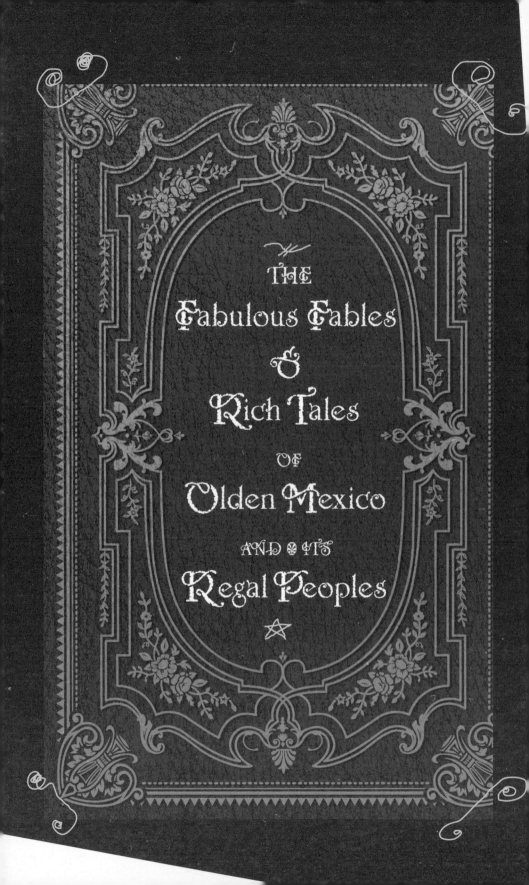

THE

Fabulous Fables

&

Rich Tales

OF

Olden Mexico

AND OF ITS

Regal Peoples

n the beginning there was only the land. A great land that stretched on and on as far as the eye could see. Savage dinosaurs roamed the earth unaware they were even in Mexico, for it did not exist as a country then. Thunderous fights occurred between mighty sauropods and crafty spinosaurs. It was a wild land full of passion and brute lust. Two hunters, Kah and Miko, cautiously walked through the forest in search of sustenance for their families. They were dressed only in small loincloths. Miko was nervous, for he had seen a herd of hadrosaurs not far from where they made camp the night before. Neither hunter, although they were skilled in hand-to-hand combat, was a match for a hadrosaur. The two hunters were tired. It had been a long day and they had come up empty. Soon the rainy season would be upon them and it would be time for the great migration. Kah was the stronger of the two. He reached out his arm and rested it on Miko's shoulder. It was a reassuring touch for Miko. He had been worried that they would find no food. Kah wanted Miko to not worry. He suggested they make camp and went about finding kindling for a fire. The two men did their tasks with well-rehearsed precision and soon they had a suitable camp. They had hunted in these pre-Mexican woods often. As the blazing hot sun sank into the blue mountains outside of current-day Mexico City, Kah once again put his hand out to reassure Miko that everything would be all right. He rested it on Miko's bare shoulder. Miko could feel the big man's hand on his shoulder and felt comforted by it. Kah then slid his hand along Miko's muscular back, stopping right before his firm buns. Miko instinctively stepped away but Kah held him and pulled him in. Within seconds the stronger man was pressing his hungry lips onto his friend. Miko struggled to get free but Kah was strong. He held Miko in a tight hug and now both his hands firmly held the smaller man's round buttocks. Miko was terrified and strangely aroused at the same time. He had often stayed awake dreaming about what the big man would feel like and now it was actually happening! As Kah pulled Miko into his broad muscular chest Miko could feel his willpower draining. He would give over to his desire once and for all—but suddenly there was a great crashing in the forest. A *Tyrannosaurus rex* burst through the trees and wrapped his mighty and awesome jaws around Kah and snapped his body in half. These were dangerous times. They were the best of times if you could avoid the dinosaurs but the worst of times if you could not. Miko never could erase the image of his friend mercilessly slung back and forth like a rag doll in the mouth of that *Tyrannosaurus*. He hiked back to his village and became known as Mikothelan, lord emperor of the Incas.

The Incas were the first inhabitants of Mexico. Where they originally came from remains a mystery. Many historians believe aliens brought the Incas here from a planet outside of our solar system, so if you were thinking Mars or even Pluto, think again; you're way off. I'm not buying it! Aliens did not bring the Incas to this planet. The Incas were just too dumb. More than likely, as more and more research demonstrates, the Incas probably just grew up in Mexico naturally and built some cities and lived good lives, occasionally eaten by dinosaurs. There really isn't much we can learn from these people. They weren't cavemen but they weren't rocket scientists either. They enjoyed about a million years of peace and tranquility and then the Mayans came, and that's when the shit hit the fan.

The Mayans probably were brought here by aliens. They were too smart to be born in Mexico. They invented a calendar. A calendar? Really? That's not something you invent every day if you're born in Mexico. They "built" pyramids. Right! Earthlings living in mud huts built pyramids. Sorry, not buying it. The Mayans were definitely aliens. They were much more civilized than the Incas. They wore suits and went to work and made up games like football played in giant stadiums. I once had the opportunity to visit one of their stadiums. Not really that great but considering it was built by people whose average height was two and a half feet, you can't help but tip your hat to the Mayan people. They slaughtered the Incas in no time flat. They took them from their houses and whacked their heads off and used the whacked-off heads in their football games. (Don't worry, they get what's coming to them later. What goes around comes around.) They built great cities and established trade routes. They grew as a race and were said to be numbered in the millions. Their king, Esteban, was considered to be a god. Scholars now believe that he had contact with the aliens and so he had more knowledge than everyone else, but this is only reasonable speculation. What we do know is that he was a boastful and proud man who ruled with an iron fist. He had been a great footballer in his day and a star athlete in the school system. If my reading of the Florentine Codex is correct, then he studied law and went on to marry a woman with great wealth. (Not too bad on the eyes either!) With her wealth and his natural good looks and grace they quickly climbed the ladder of success in the backstabbing, drama-filled world of the Mayan court. They were natural-born politicians, so when election time came rolling around they had run such a smooth campaign that they easily had the votes to be declared the new king and queen. They would stay atop the throne for many a year until a politician so smooth and fun to be around, the kind of guy you would drink a beer with, entered the city and won the hearts of everybody.

Montezuma grew up in the farming community outside of Tijuana. He wasn't a Mayan but an Aztec. He had wanted to be a town planner and to some degree that's what he was—maybe the greatest town planner in history. He built Mexico in a few weeks. He was no Thomas Jefferson, mind you, but he was pretty good. Jefferson was our greatest thinker when it came to cultivating the land. He understood the delicate balance between the growth of civilization and croppery. I consider myself a gentleman farmer in the Jeffersonian sense. Before I was asked to leave San Luis Obispo I had a nice half acre of land with about a hundred head of donkey. They were a stubborn lot of animals and a half acre inside the town limits is not enough land for them to really stretch out on. They needed way more land and way more food than I supplied. A day didn't go by without a donkey in my kitchen. They ate me out of house and home until Baxter talked them into making a break for it. They stampeded through San Luis Obispo and headed up into the Sierra Nevada mountains. Technically, by California law, I still own them, but I'm happy enough to let them roam free.

Montezuma had bigger fish to fry than donkeys! He marched into the town where the Mayans were and quickly set up shop as the new guy in town. He was a cool customer from what we historians know. He had the ladies dripping wet with his handsome looks and self-confident attitude. In no time at all he was the most popular guy in the region. Archaeologists claim he loved the ladies. He had many wives of all shapes and sizes, although legend has it that he enjoyed huge knockers. If you go to certain areas in Mexico today women with really big jugs are said to have "Montezuma's Bazumas." I think there's a limit to how big a set of breasts should be. Some of the women in Mexico have tits way out to here—floppy big'ns that make them so top-heavy it looks like they are going to fall over. No thank you, Mr. Montezuma, you can keep your size 50 E-cups for yourself; I like mine big, but not THAT big. If I'm going to have a pair of boobs jangling in my face I don't want them to threaten me with suffocation! I like to get my hands on 'em and enjoy the ride.

Under Montezuma, Mexico and the new Aztec empire grew to magnificent splendor and opulence. Gold adorned every woman who walked the golden streets. Elaborate parties were given every night, with giant ice sculptures and fountains of hot gold. The excess saw no boundaries, for these were the "go-go" years, when everyone overextended themselves and cheap credit was the name of the game. On the top of this all-too-fragile wealth and lavish lifestyle sat Montezuma without a care in the world.

Meanwhile, a million miles away in Spain, at the court of Fernando Valenzuela, a young, handsome adventurer by the name of Hernán Cortés was dreaming big and shooting for the stars. Valenzuela had just granted the stout explorer a legion of ships and casks of red wine to set sail for Mexico in search of gold. Cortés was a hard man. His chiseled features and rugged good looks suggested a soldier of fortune, which he was, but he turned out to be much more than that. He was a conqueror of lands and a loyal subject to the queen of Spain. He was also a ruthless bully who tamed a people and forged a destiny for Mexico that would last even to this day. He set sail on Tuesday, July 5, 1776, unaware that a far greater country than his own had just declared its independence. The ships were stocked with casks of red wine and goblets for drinking. For drinking fine red wine was the sailor's life in olden times. Also each man had his own broadsword made from the finest iron ore mined in deepest, blackest Africa. These swords were so great they often were named. Names like La Legion, Excelsior, Magnifico, El Cartagena, Beatrice, Fontanello and Esmeralda ring out among broadsword collectors far and wide. At the Sword and Shield, a high-end-replica sword shop specializing in rapiers and broadswords, a group of us meet once a month to discuss these ancient weapons. We often make up our own wondrous deeds done by these legendary swords. I have several replicas and I've created histories for them that I enjoy telling to people if they're over at the house. Cortés sailed with many fine broadswords and horses and leather and casks of red wine. The wine poured down the Spaniards' bearded faces under the hot sun but they had not a care in the world, for soon they would be in Mexico with all the gold they desired.

Montezuma, the dumb Aztec, never knew what hit him. Cortés was a man who knew what he wanted and he just reached out and grabbed it. He had a lust for life and he showed it. Using his broadsword, Gabriella, he cut a hole through Mexico, hacking and chopping off faces and limbs and enjoying his red wine with a hearty laugh. The smell of sweaty leather and dried wine hung in the air like the smell of sex in a whorehouse. Soon all of Mexico would smell of the Spaniards, and they would like it. Pungent were the days of Cortés! His men were ripe with lusty doings and bold adventure. They had hearty laughs and enjoyed roasted mutton chops dripping with olive oil. They would just toss the uneaten parts of the mutton in the street like they didn't care. They were a band of brothers known only as "the Conquistadors" and they were the true Mexicans. Their more handsome European looks were an instant draw for all of the Aztecs and the Mayans, who were not a great-looking race, but they had one problem. Although not much scientific record exists concerning penis size, we can judge by ancient Aztec drawings and paintings that the Aztec people had huge penises. Some of them appeared to be two feet long! With that kind of size, how could any man compete for a woman's affection? The Conquistadors quickly realized they would have to cut off every penis bigger than their own in the land. If we can believe oral history, this period was called the Time of the Great Castrata! Soon the Aztec women forgot their desire for giant penises and settled into comfortable lives with the much smaller Spaniards. But could a memory be extinguished so easily? Hardly. It explains why even to this day Mexican women secretly lust after that which they lost, a truly giant penis.

But who was their leader? Who was Hernán Cortés? And how did Maximilian get into this picture? Read on, dear reader, for more glory and excellence follows in chapter 2 of *The Fabulous Fables and Rich Tales of Olden Mexico and Its Regal Peoples*.

## END OF CHAPTER ONE

# *My Favorite Doodles*

Doodles are a unique form of expression for me. A way to release stress and clear my mind . . . and if I don't say so myself, some of these are pretty darn good.

"Alien"

One of the friendly aliens who brought the Mayans to Mexico. Possibly named Glabbo.

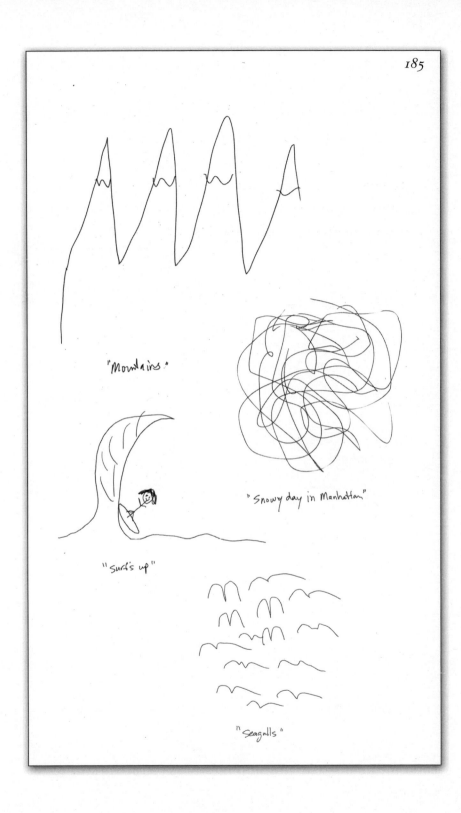

"Mountains"

"Snowy day in Manhattan"

"Surf's up"

"Seagulls"

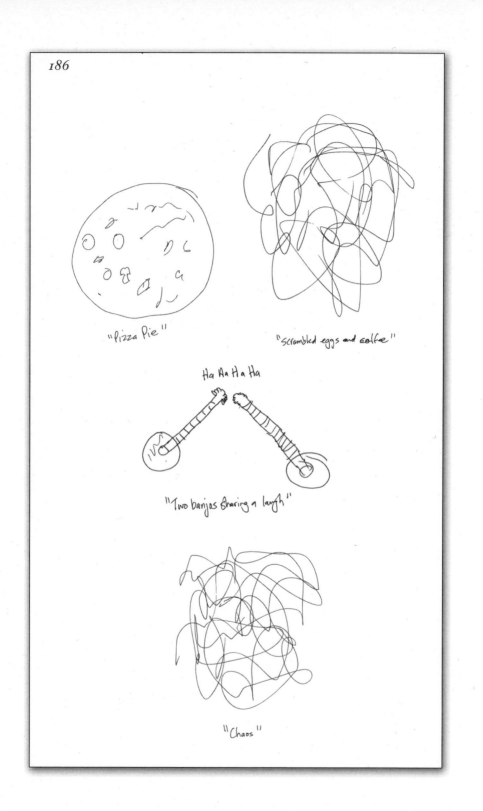

"Pizza Pie"

"Scrambled eggs and coffee"

Ha Ha Ha Ha

"Two banjos sharing a laugh"

"Chaos"

# I DISH THE DIRT!

I've enjoyed a great life with many friends and wonderful acquaintances. My time in local news and cable TV gave me great access to personalities from every walk of life. Far be it from me to turn this noble chronicle of my life into a smut-filled smear campaign against those who confided in me over the years, but I will not stand by and allow these same people to drag my name through the mud without putting up a fight. Even if they haven't tried to bring me down, I know that's what they're thinking and I'm a firm believer in the preemptive strike. If it's good for American foreign policy, which clearly it has proven to be, then it's good for Ron Burgundy.

For starters, just to put to rest a rumor floating around, I did make love to Katie Couric. It was wonderfully slow and

filled with passion. This was about two months ago. Veronica
and I had rented a secluded cabin up in the Finger Lakes dis-
trict in upstate New York. Nights were alive with the sounds
of crickets and cicadas and the trees bending in the breeze.
You could hear the gentle lapping of the water on the hulls of
the boats across the lake. It was like we'd stepped into a more
genteel time. It was the kind of peace we both desperately
needed. I spent my days relaxing by the lake and my nights on
the porch with my pipe and brandy and my best girl. On the
third day we were awakened by a thunderous sound explod-
ing across the lake. I took out my binoculars, and by the teat
of Arachne, what did I see? It was Katie Couric in a cigarette
boat called the *Blazin' Bitch* bouncing over the water. I knew
that she was a bit of a tramp, but this was a ridiculous breach
of decorum! I got in my golf cart (everyone up at the lake has
a golf cart, okay?) and I drove around the lake to the dock.
Sure enough, Katie roars in, paying no attention to the "no
wake" signs, and as she's coming into her mooring she sees me
and starts waving. "Ron! Ronny! Ronny! It's meeeeee, Katie."

Knock me down with a feather! I come all the way over
ready to chew her a new one and gosh darn it if she isn't the
cutest little bug there is. She just radiates health and beauty. I
can't help it. Every time I see Katie Couric my insides just go
to mush. I don't know what to say. . . . I manage a "Hi, Katie,
it's me, Ron Burgundy." She laughs and then yells back, "Get
over here, you dog. I have some Natty Lights in the cooler
down below." So next thing you know I'm making my way
across the deck of the *Blazin' Bitch* and heading for the cabin.
Katie's about ten steps ahead of me. When I get down into the

cabin she's got a marijuana cigarette and a bottle of Captain Morgan spiced rum in her hand. The whole cabin is upholstered in Ed Hardy–tooled leather. John Mayer is piped in over a built-in Bose sound system. "Money. Makes it all happen, right, Ronny?" she says to me.

"So I've been coming up to the lake for a while now and I haven't seen you before," I venture.

"Shit, Burgs, I just go where the *Blazin' Bitch* takes me."

"Where's your new fiancé?" I ask.

"We all gotta break away, right, Ron?" And then she puts her foot on my crotch. And that's as far as I'm going to take this tale. There's still a little friction over this incident in the Burgundy household. Besides, I've never been one to kiss and tell—but since there was no time for kissing, suffice it to say Katie Couric is a real wildcat with an insatiable desire to be loved, and I loved her. Enough said.

What else . . .

George Stephanopoulos wears women's underwear when he delivers the news. There is absolutely nothing intriguing or interesting about him at all except for this strange anomaly. Is it sexual? Is it wrapped up in some kind of identity crisis? Is he a thrill seeker? Nope to all three. He just confided in me that wearing women's panties while delivering the news lets him stay in touch with his feminine side. He also said women's underwear is made from softer materials and it feels better on his ball sack.

Or here's one . . .

If you remember the Captain from Captain and Tennille, he's always claimed he wasn't a real captain, but hold the boat! He *was* a captain. I was on board the *Angelica Nora* when he quite drunkenly guided it into some rocks off the coast of South America. The rusty old ship was overladen with stolen Chinese art and an assortment of international spies. I had agreed to work in the engine room in return for passage home to San Diego. How I got to China is a whole other book. Anyway, we spent the nights on deck drinking rum until we passed out. The Captain—his real name is Daryl Dragon but he went by Scardworth in those days—left the navigation of the ship to his pet seal. I know it sounds ridiculous, like I'm making the whole thing up, but seals make great navigators. This seal, Stinky was his name, just happened to be unfamiliar with the Southern Hemisphere and he got confused. When the Captain woke up he thought we were coming into San Francisco when in fact we were off the coast of Peru. Those are some of the toughest waters to navigate for seal or man and, well, Scardworth wasn't up to it. We hit rock and tore up the hull good. Only the Captain and I survived the sinking. In the lifeboat he tried to eat me but I grew to like him anyway. I told him his secret was safe with me but I warned him never to become a captain again. I guess the pull was just too great.

Maybe I shouldn't but what the heck. . . .

Vice President Walter Mondale and I ran a cockfighting ring for six years. I was just starting out in the news and he was the attorney general for the state of Minnesota. He used state funds to buy an old twin-engine mail plane, which he flew down to El Paso, where we had our ring. We ran twenty fights every Friday and Saturday night. He bred his own gamecocks, cut off the comb and wattle himself to prepare them for the fights and raked in a small fortune. He named his best cock "Sir Humphrey," after his good friend Hubert Humphrey. Sir Humphrey still holds the record for consecutive kills at 947. He was almost more eagle than rooster. He remains a legend in cockfighting lore to this day. There's an old Mexican-style *corrido* that goes,

> Sir Humphrey, Sir Humphrey
> Has entered the ring
> No one can beat him
> For he is the king
> His beak is a razor
> His feet are like knives
> He's come from the devil
> To take God from our lives.

It was used for many years to scare Mexican children into eating their vegetables. Anyway Walter Mondale loved Sir Humphrey. We both cried the day we ate him.

Now you got me going, so why not spill the beans about this. . . .

There was a time when Warren Beatty, the movie actor, was quite promiscuous. It's the truth. I know what you're thinking—not Warren Beatty! No way! From what I have heard from very reliable sources he would use his good looks and Hollywood power to attract women into the bedroom. Yes, that Warren Beatty. Get over it. He would meet them at parties or while shooting his movies and take it from there.

Believe me, I was as shocked as anybody when I first heard this, but apparently it's true. I guess you can't judge a book by its cover! I've known some promiscuous men in my time—Brian Fantana, World B. Free and of course myself come to mind—but Warren Beatty? Who would have guessed it?

The stupid old urban legend about Elton John collapsing after a concert and having a gallon of semen pumped from his stomach never seems to die, but I can say with complete certainty that this never happened. I have made an in-depth study of this ridiculous semen-swallowing legend and those falsely accused of it, and I can tell you there are only eleven people who have swallowed more than twelve ounces of semen and had their stomachs pumped because of it. They are: Rod Stewart, David Bowie, Duane Allman, Jeff Beck, Jon Bon Jovi, Andy Warhol, Britney Spears, Tonya Harding, Dick Cheney, Andy Roddick and Anita Bryant. Let the rumors about others stop! This is the complete list as it stands today. We need to set the record straight on this story. It's important news and we have to get it right.

Here's some investigative reporting. . . . After Barbra Streisand ended her relationship with Elliott Gould she carried on a yearlong, torrid affair with a young news reporter then anchoring KNBC-TV in Los Angeles by the name of Tom Brokaw. You heard it here! Fantana and I got the scoop from Ted Koppel, who was jealous of Brokaw's success at the time. News Anchors can be pretty catty and we knew it. To corroborate, because after all I am an investigative journalist, I broke into Streisand's room at the Beverly Hilton and snuck under the bed with a tape recorder and a typewriter. I waited patiently for six or seven hours but then got hungry and left. Meanwhile Fantana spotted the two lovers in the Sportsmen's Lodge over in the San Fernando Valley. We then decided to disguise ourselves as an out-of-town married couple on our second honeymoon. We checked into the Sportsmen's Lodge, with Fantana as my wife, and set about looking like a normal older married couple. We sat by the pool, went to the breakfast nook and spent our evenings at the bar. Bob Hope was there every night with a different lady, of course, but that was hardly news. No, we were onto something big. The Vietnam War was still happening and the military was in the middle of the Tet Offensive, but what we had on our hands was the kind of news you dream about as a young reporter but know will never happen. Ed Harken was furious with Fantana and me. He was yelling at us to get back to San Diego and report on the war—but of course he didn't know the dynamite we were sitting on. So one night after about two weeks of surveillance, we see them. We're posing as this innocent couple from Decatur, Illinois, and Fantana, dressed as my wife, runs up to Barbra and asks her for her autograph. While he's making small talk about recipes I slip into their room and place a tape recorder under the bed. The whole thing went off without a hitch. The first half of the tape is just a lot of mumbling and squeaking bedsprings, but then there was this:

**Barbra**
**Tom, I can't do this anymore.**

**Tom**
**Why? Why not?**

**Barbra**

I won't be a home wrecker. You love your wife. This is nuts!

**Tom**

I've explained it over and over again. I've got too much passion in me for one woman. Don't you see I need you and Joey? [He was having an affair with Joey Heatherton at the same time.]

**Barbra**

I need more. I need a man who will be there for me.

**Tom**

I'm here. I'm right here, baby.

**Barbra**

Tuesdays and Sundays! It's not enough, Tom. I want love. Love like you read about in the dime-store books.

**Tom**

I'll leave my wife. I'll go on the road with you. I'll learn to sing or dance. I could be in the chorus.

**Barbra**

It would never work. You would only resent me.

**Tom**

Oh, Barbra!

**Barbra**

I need you to know something else.

**Tom**

You're cheating on me?

**Barbra**

No, of course not. You need to know I'm pregnant with our child.

**Tom**

Nuh-uh! No way! Couldn't be mine—you're pretty loose, you know—I'm guessing there's been a lot of guys—could have been Donald Sutherland. There's just a lot of guys. NO WAY! I'm not responsible for nothing! Not a chance. Don't put this shit on me, Barbra.

**Barbra**

Don't worry, Tom. It's okay. No one will ever know. I want to have the baby. I'll put her up for adoption and the two of us can watch over her. We can see to it that she gets breaks in this world, breaks she might not even deserve, but we'll look after her. She will be a living testament to our secret love.

**Tom**

That is beautiful. Barbra, I will always love you. One more time for old times' sake.

Then the bed starts squeaking again for about another two hours. We had it. The biggest scoop in decades. We were sure to get the Pulitzer. We drove back to San Diego with the evidence but somewhere along the freeway Fantana and I made a big decision that has affected the news business ever since.

We decided that this was a private matter between Brokaw and Streisand and it really wasn't news. It was a huge shift in the way we, and ultimately America, thought about news. Our decision and subsequent focus on hard news rippled across the country until Americans simply lost their taste for salacious gossip and celebrity news. One more thing about this story. The love child? Her name is Jennifer Aniston and she is America's sweetheart.

## MY NEIGHBOR: BREAKING NEWS

I spent the night in jail. As you know, I've been at war with my neighbor Richard Wellspar over my leaf blower. He borrowed it and then never returned it. It's been three weeks. Enough said. Anyway I crashed his little block party yesterday. I brought some very interesting pictures of his girlfriend, Cynthia Spaller. I had some old photos of her I took on a boat nearly thirty years ago. Bob Guccione would have paid me American money for them, if you know what I mean. So I start passing the photos out to everyone there, moms, dads, children, etc., and Wellspar flips his lid!

"Burgundy, this is the last straw!" he yells. "This woman is my wife!" (That I did not know, but I'll admit it: Sometimes I can be pretty unobservant.)

"Well, this woman and I did stuff on a boat that everyone needs to know about!" I yelled back.

"I'm calling the police!"

"Not before I make it plain to everyone at this party that

your wife, Cynthia Spaller, and I did stuff in every position imaginable with absolutely no regard for safety for hours and hours. We did not make love! We did it like zoo monkeys with no compassion and no end in sight but multiple dumb orgasms. It was debasing and humiliating and we enjoyed it! That is all. My name is Ron Burgundy."

I stormed out of there, only slowing down to key his car. I did spend the night in jail but I think he got the point. He won't be borrowing anything of mine anytime soon!

# THE REST OF THE STORY: THE NINETIES

Of course in writing a novel about my life I realize that much of my story has already been told. I've starred in two factual documentaries about myself. The first one I titled *Anchorman: The Legend of Ron Burgundy*. It covered a period in the news business of great change. It was the battle of the sexes, and you know what? . . . We all won! It's a better world with female anchormen. It also was a delightful retelling of my courtship with the lovely Veronica Corningstone, who then later became my wife and the woman I do it with. The documentary was a great success enjoyed by billions of people across the world and it quickly spawned a sequel, which reveals an even more adventurous time for me. I've titled this one *Anchorman 2: The Legend Continues.* This documentary also covers a game-changing moment in the history of tele-vised news reporting, namely the epoch of twenty-four-hour cable news. As both these documentaries do an excellent job of chronicling my life in those tumultuous eras, I see no rea-son to waste the reader's time with descriptions of what they can see in color for a few bucks extra. I highly recommend *Anchorman 2: The Legend Continues.* It's very accurate. We stuck to the facts with no bullshit. I tip my hat to the filmmakers and my own acting ability. I'm no film critic writing for one of these vitally important Internet blogs, but I will say it may just be the finest film ever made. It bears a second and third screening to be sure, for there are many nuances that are only enriched by multiple viewings. These two documenta-ries combined with the facts I've presented in this book form an accurate picture of my life up to a certain point. I shall not embellish on the years covered in the documentaries other than to say documentaries are not a complete life! During that whole period I ate cereal, I blew my nose, I shit my pants, I costarred in a movie with Sylvester Stallone called *Over the Top* and I went to the grocery store. So much of life is not worth spinning into tales that we forget that tales themselves are little more than omissions of choice. For instance, during the period chronicled in *Anchorman: The Legend of Ron Bur-gundy,* Brian Fantana and I ran a very successful car-detailing shop in San Diego. This was in the original thousand-page script, along with a very funny story about the day I bought a comb that then broke. Well, some of this delightful storytelling just had to be omitted in the interest of time. The comb story was a real doozy and if I ever get a chance to do a documentary about that alone I will take that opportunity, but you know what they say about letting go of things you love in a script: "When in Rome."

Sadly even here in this sweeping tale of my many adventures and wonderful deeds I am forced to omit details in the interest of space. What needs to be told and what needs to be left out? People still want to know where I was the night of the O. J. Simpson conspiracy. I have some details that would shed new light on the whole mix-up. Is it worth throwing in here? Did I barter a peace between Bears quarterback Jim McMahon and Commissioner Pete Rozelle? Was I best man at the wedding of Sean Penn and Madonna? Did I squeak some bedsprings in the Ozarks with a governor's wife by the name of Hillary? I mean, what is a good story and what is just more stuff that happened? In point of fact there's a good story everywhere you look. During a short separation from my wife and sex friend, Veronica, I took a run at every Spice Girl. I'm not the kind of guy to kiss and tell but Scary Spice was the very best in the sack and aptly named. I was terrified and aroused the whole time. I invented the Wonderbra and the Super Soaker on the same day. I was minutes away from preventing the whole Chernobyl disaster while doing work for the State Department in Russia. Is that a story or is that just a guy doing his job? Anyway, you can see my problem here. What stands out?

One thing comes to mind I've never talked about. In fact I've never written a word about it for fear of reprisals. I did some government work in the early nineties for George Herbert Walker Bush. I'll admit that politically we didn't always align but I'm nothing if not patriotic, and when the president calls on you to do a job, well then you do it and you don't ask questions. You just do it. You blindly march into battle because he's the president. That's just what being an American is all about, my friends.

Because I was such good friends with Manuel Noriega, the leader of Panama, Bush 1 asked if I could broker a deal between Noriega and the U.S. This was before Operation Just Cause, which sent twenty-four thousand troops down into Panama to broker a different kind of deal. Before that deal, which wasn't really a deal at all but just a military invasion to take over a country, there was a much more complicated deal involving ███████████, Noriega, Saddam Hussein and Margaret Thatcher. I flew to Panama, where I had a summer house near the palace and where I enjoyed the bounty that came with being great buddies with the misunderstood Noriega. While in his company I was to offer him ███████████████████████, among other things, including a Land Rover with custom Kenneth Cole leather seats. To help navigate the complexities of the deal I was accompanied by Secretary of Defense Richard Bruce "Dick" Cheney. I did not like him. From the very beginning we fought. There was something so cold and calculating about the man that I immediately sized him up as a world-class idiot who was surely going to blow the whole thing. His judgment in all matters of foreign policy was counterintuitive to natural reason. For instance, in a meeting with Saddam Hussein, Cheney suggested

███████████████ █████████████████████████ loved
boiled eggs██████████████████████████. Thatcher was
insufferable; she insisted that ████████████████████
████████████████████████████ at an advance show-
ing of *The Bodyguard* with singer/songwriter Dolly Parton
and King Fahd. Also present were General Norman Schwarzkopf, VP Dan Quayle, rock guitarist and presidential adviser
Ted Nugent, ████████████ and myself. The meeting was a
lively one, with ██████████████████████████ as a
suggestion. Pat Robertson, who was also in attendance, indi-
cated that he would ██████████████████████████
██████████████████ several other S & M followers
███████████████ ██████████████████████████
Glenn Miller ████████████████████████ having
███████████ wistful ████████████████████
██████████████████████████ forty kilos of Panama-
nian ████████████ ███████████████
██████████████ because Thatcher loved the smell of it.
I was taken to a room in Kuwait with a hood over my head.
I knew that Soviet general secretary Mikhail Gorbachev was
going to play ball but I also knew that I had to act fast. I handed
over ██████████████████████████████! I
couldn't believe it! Dan Quayle, probably one of the hand-
somest politicians I've ever met and a great doubles tennis partner, was behind the clandestine handoff from the
beginning. He was carrying the briefcase with ████████.
How Ted Nugent gained such access was not my concern,
but Thatcher said, "███████████ went ███████████ fifteen ██████████████████████ hammerhead sharks

██████████████████████████████ dead with one word. A chill went through the room. Only Dick Cheney was laughing. Noriega looked sweaty and I felt sorry for him. I gave over my package to ████████████. We got on a plane, James Baker and I, and flew to Saudi Arabia, where Afghan freedom fighter and American ally Osama bin Laden were waiting with ████████████████. We went out to dinner. James Baker ordered the ██████████████. I must say I've never been one for Mexican food in foreign countries. If you're going to have Mexican food it's best in America. The conversation centered on ██████████ in ████████████████. Bush had agreed to ████████████ without reservation. ██████████████ any ██████████████████████████ before ██████████ ██████ Runnin' Rebels Greg Anthony and Stacey Augmon. Fahd, of course, was a huge booster for UNLV basketball and a personal friend of Jerry Tarkanian. This was all going nowhere fast and I had had enough. I called Dick Cheney from ████████████████. He was not happy and he let me know it. "If you can't ████████████████ patriot ████████████ water-board ███████████████████ American way of life ████████████████████ my legacy ██████████████████████████ to buy Liz a toaster oven. Son of a bitch, Burgundy, I thought we had a deal." And then he hung up. It was the loneliest I've ever felt. To be stranded in Kuwait holding all that ████████████. I went to Noriega and warned him. Thatcher would ████████████████ Harrier Jump Jets ██████████ nuts ██████████ Armen Gilliam as well. I knew if the press got ahold of this they would have a field day. It put me in quite a bind as a committed journalist. I had the entire three-hundred-page brief in my hotel room. I was asked to ██████████ not because but ██████████ Parton's song ██████████████████ nudity included. The ██████████ glass ██████████. "Holy balls!" I shouted. "Is this where ██████████?" ██████████ but Schwarzkopf tried to take a swing at him and I stepped in. The outcome was ██████████ mission ██████████ not in the Bush library. ██████████████████ paper-shredding machine on the eighth floor running nonstop for days. CIA operative ██████████ stepped in to ██████████ gloves ██████████ disposed of the ██████████ like lumpy soup ██████████ field of un-marked graves. That's where it turned. Suddenly I was in real danger. It's a feeling I cultivate. Like sexual pleasure, danger sets off certain life-affirming emotions in me. I quickly sprang into action. The drugs were in my suitcase. The money was in the hands of ██████████. ██████████████████ ██████████████████ wet ██████████ *New York Times* ██████████████████ firing at me and Jerry Tarkanian. The plane was one hundred yards away. Dolly Parton and ██████████ heels and red leather ██████████. I hadn't even flown before but there I was in the plane with ██████████, Cheney, Thatcher and ██████████. Back in the States I locked the documents in a private vault I had hidden under an auto junkyard outside of Gary, Indiana. I believe in transparency. I believe we the peo-ple should know what our leaders are up to when it comes to vitally important foreign policy. Now the story can be told, and let the consequences fall where they may. If ████████████ ██████████ grapes in the ole basket!

Throughout the rest of the nineties I turned more and more toward investigative news. I hosted an hour of television on PBS called *The Burgundy Journal.* The whole news team stayed together as we tackled big subjects well beyond our ken. We were out of our league over there on PBS. There were guys in the mailroom who knew more about the state of the world than any of us. So we told the news the only way we knew how: directly, forcefully and without substance. It was, as always, a hit. The highest-rated show in the history of PBS. Unfortunately the pay was ridiculous. Champ had more restaurant ambitions. Brick wanted to run around on grass and I was beginning to feel like an old man in a young man's game. After about a half a year of *The Burgundy Journal* I retired from the news business and walked away on top—a champion and a winner, the number one guy of all time.

A couple of years later I received the highest honor any News Anchor can be awarded—the Golden Anchor. It was usually reserved for network anchormen, but it was only fitting that after a career unmatched by anyone's I should receive this prestigious award. They all came: Cronkite, Jennings, Curtis, Brokaw, Rather, Sawyer, Mantooth, Couric, Lehrer. The room was filled with news greats. A lot of scores that had gone unsettled got settled that night. I wasn't able to even get to my thank-you speech before a fight broke out between Rather and Koppel that then grew to a regular old-fashioned donnybrook. Tables flew, chairs broke, bottles were smashed, machetes were drawn, shots were fired—it was the most fun I'd had in years. It seemed fitting that the night should progress into a good old-fashioned news fight. It seemed more fitting that in the end only four men were standing over the broken bodies piled up in the room. I looked around to survey the wreckage and a smile came to my bloodied face. There beside me was my old news team, triumphant again, standing tall and victorious over the battlefield.

# HOW TO RELATE
# TO CHILDREN

As a father I've experienced many ups and downs raising
a child. Parenting can give us so much joy. To see the wonder
in a child's eyes is as close to heaven as I've ever come. (I'm
speaking metaphorically of course. Physically I've come very
close to heaven, as I was on the summit of Mount Kilimanjaro
with game show host Gene Rayburn and Beatle Ringo Starr.)
There can also be great dissatisfaction when it comes to children. I've had interactions with them that have left me feeling
sad and alienated and hollow inside, to the point of wanting
to kill myself. If you're not careful a child can spin you into a
suicidal drain from which only pills and sex and circus rides

can save you. Their brains are mysterious puzzles that con-
found all human reasoning. I've been very frustrated talking
to children and I'll admit it, I'm always a little terrified of
them. If you get in a room alone with one you can't help but
start thinking about how irrational they are. It's only a matter
of time before you begin to wonder if they are going to attack
you or start flying around the room or speak backward. I was
locked in a room with a small girl one time who started to
speak backward. I nearly fainted but summoned the courage
to try and kill her. I was moving toward her with that intent
when the child's mother entered the room and stopped me.
She explained that they were from Poland and the child was
trying to talk to me in Polish. I guess they speak backward in
Poland. My point here is that children say and do stuff that
makes no sense. It can be very unsettling. I keep a candy bar
in every room in my house just in case I'm left alone with a
child. So how do you relate to a creature that lives by no rules?

Every summer for one week I run something called Camp
Ronny. I get a bunch of poor kids from broken homes and bad
neighborhoods and take them out into the woods for some
hot dogs and sing-alongs. It's my way of giving back. There's
only one rule at Camp Ronny, and that rule is, have fun!
Many of the kids come from environments where they hardly
ever just have fun. The first day I teach them some basic Boy
Scout/American Indian stuff like making smoke signals and
tying knots. Boys and girls just love this kind of outdoor fun.
On the third day they are on their own. They have to make
their own shelters, forage for food, make tools and fire. The
little ones, in the eight-to-nine-year range, always have prob-

lems with this, but eventually they get it. When they see I'm not going to help them they get it. Over the years we've had some close calls with some of the children and animals. Some nosey child welfare do-gooders have shared their opinions with me about Camp Ronny, but I'll tell you what, many of these kids go on to become prominent wrestlers, stockbrokers, Realtors and bouncers. Do these children become part of our great social fabric that ties us all together? No, but that wasn't going to happen anyway. What I've done is instilled in them a ruthless instinct for survival at all costs. Kids who come out of Camp Ronny are some of the scariest and worst citizens in the country. Famous alumni include Kenneth Lay, Sean Hannity, Junkyard Dog, King Kong Bundy, Paul Wolfowitz and Laura Ingraham. They may be hated and feared by regular Americans but they are survivors, and that's what's important.

If you can instill a little confidence in a child, then you've gone a long way to being a great parent. A ten-year-old will feel on top of the world if you can teach them to drive on a freeway. From what I understand the Chinese allow their children to operate heavy machinery making garments and fabricating car parts at a very young age. This must do gangbusters for their confidence!

Apart from that there's not much more I can say about relating to children. Scientifically speaking the medulla oblongata of children is smaller than that of adults, and so that's something I'm sure.

## MY NEIGHBOR: MY BAD

Weird development in the whole Richard Wellspar affair. I found my Craftsman leaf blower in my garage sitting on the workbench with a plate of cookies and a very nice handwritten note dated a month ago. Can you believe it? He must have returned it the day I lent it to him! What a goof. My bad. Sometimes life gets silly. Only in San Diego, folks, only in San Diego.

# WHERE I'M AT TODAY

Don't you worry, life's pretty good for Ron Burgundy these days. It was touch-and-go there for a little while but counting my chips, I see I came out the big winner. When all is said and done I will walk away from the poker table of life richer than when I came in—except I will be dead, which in many ways is not richer than when I came in. Someone once said one day we all end up at the banquet of our own consequences. For many men that banquet is an unsettling and fitting end to a life of poor choices. For me I'm at the banquet of my consequences and there's roast beef and mutton chops and red wine and cheeses and pancakes and a stack of Heath bars and creamed corn and succulent other foods like shrimp cocktail, hot dogs with sauerkraut, ravioli and three-bean salad,

to name a few more—ice cream too—anyway it's quite a banquet, really, and it's all consequences of a life well lived. But it
didn't feel that way a few years back and I'll tell you why.

In 2004 I was basically retired. My day consisted of a round
of golf with Merlin Olsen, a five-dollar lunch at China Buffet,
some checkers with Captain Willoby Faloon, a few personal
appearances and then home for dinner. If I was lucky, and
frankly I'm always lucky, I got some you-know-what from Mrs.
Burgundy. She's still got it. Even at our advanced age we can
still do stuff that would make a Nevada prostitute sit up and
take notice. Anyway, that's how a typical day went before the
fall of 2004. Somehow through one of my many personal appearances I got involved with a gentleman by the name of Fast
Eddy Keel. People in and around San Diego know the name
and face of Fast Eddy as it appeared on many bus stop seats
advertising home loans. He approached me early in 2004 with
an opportunity too good for me to pass up. I've never been
one to try and profit from my name unless there's money in
it, but here was a case that spoke to a particular passion of
mine—namely building a high-end gated housing community. The Burgundy Estates, as they later were so named,
was to be an ambitious housing development of fine homes
heavily guarded and protected from the disintegrating social
contract threatening our way of life. Each home would have
fifteen rooms, including a screening room and a great room;
a granite-topped kitchen; huge stainless appliances; a four-
car garage; two swimming pools; a guesthouse; an indoor
rock-climbing wall; an old-timey "make your own sundae" ice-
cream parlor; his-and-her walk-in closets; koi ponds in every

room—in short, only the best! Not to mention all the gadgets and gizmos the world had to offer at that time. Land clearing and building started in the spring of 2005. Each house was presold at about $2.5 million. With thirty houses to be built Fast Eddy and I were looking at a nice tidy profit. I supervised some of the building myself. I designed the houses on cocktail napkins and scraps of paper. It was kind of an indulgence but I walked around the construction site with a hard hat on and really got to know the gang working on the houses. There was Jose, with his infectious laugh, and Hernandez the happy whistler, Manuel the prankster and Jesus and Raul and Pepe—just a buncha construction guys whose names I made up every day. Here I was, retired, in my golden years, and I should have been enjoying an easy chair and Turner Classic Movies, but instead I was hanging with the guys, pouring footings and slingin' drywall mud. I really loved it.

One day Fast Eddy comes to me and says we should do our own financing. Now, I don't have millions of dollars sitting around so the idea seemed too risky to me, but Eddy is one of those guys who has all the angles and he tells me how we could start financing the whole development with different types of loans and deferred payments. Before you know it Eddy Keel and I have a new business—Eagle-Eye Mortgage. Now, on paper Eagle-Eye had no assets whatsoever. There was only debt in the form of some questionable loans, but in 2005 debt of any kind meant one thing and one thing only—future money. In the very first year Eagle-Eye Mortgage had holdings worth two hundred million dollars. We quickly started buying up other loan operations all over San Diego and then jumped on Liberty-Cougar, the biggest home lender in the area. The new company was renamed Eagle Eye Liberty and we now had holdings valued at nearly a billion dollars. Heck, I was happy to walk around the development site with the fellas and grab a cold one after a hard day of roofing, but things began moving very fast. Eddy Keel was quite the salesman. He used to walk into laundromats in San Diego and get guys with absolutely no income to sign home loans for half a million dollars. Was it ethical? Was it the right thing to do? Anyway, Eagle Eye Liberty became Red White and Blue Lenders and then just as quickly became the American Fund, which we leveraged to buy SoCal Homestead, which later became Yankee Doodle Mortgage, which merged with Betsy Ross Financial, which had just taken over Hearth and Home Securities and became Stars and Stripes Money Tree. By early 2007 we had the biggest home mortgage company in the Southwest, servicing Southern California and Arizona. We named the company the Loan Barn. You probably remember the TV ads we did with the jingle "Need a home but you ain't got the dough? Down at the barn we never say no! The Loan Barn." We paid Donald Fagen a boatload of money to come up with that jingle! Anyway in the spring of 2008 the Loan Barn was valued at eighty billion dollars. I still didn't quite get it. I mean, I would often sit in my booth down at the Alibis with the work crew drinking my cans of Coors and think to myself, "Ron, all the money they keep saying you have is money that's in the future. Does it make sense that people are spending future money in the present? Shouldn't we wait till we get to the future to get the money and then spend it on futuristic stuff

like dino-bots and hover-cycles and phones with cameras?" I
don't know, call me old-fashioned but I like to see my money.
I always had the news station pay me in stacks of twenties. I
always bought my cars with stacks of one-dollar bills. When
someone tells me I have eighty billion dollars, I say show me
the stacks. Show me the stacks! Well, I don't need to tell you
what happened in the fall of 2008. All our future money was
deemed un-moneyable. (That's a word. No need to look it
up.) We had nothing, and what was worse, the Loan Barn
was being investigated for securities fraud, for overstating assets, for going around lending laws, blah blah blah blah, the
list of infractions went on and on. When all those loan payments came due we had to come up with eighty billion dollars. That's a lot of money. Fast Eddy Keel stayed true to his
name and beat it fast. I believe he now operates something he
calls a "party barge," which is a boat full of deviants he takes
out of Argentina into international waters for so many nefari-
ous reasons it would sicken the reader to list them, but one of
them involves cat glands and human scat. He called me one
day—he spoke fast and maybe sounded a little paranoid—
and asked if I wanted in on "the wave!" He kept saying "the
wave." And by "the wave" he meant did I want a party barge of
my own. I said no and asked him where he was and told him
that federal investigators had taken all my possessions and
were looking for him. He said he had to go and then I heard
some gunshots on his end and I haven't seen him since.

Fortunately Veronica had squirreled away some money for
us to live on and I played a hunch that put me on top once
again. After all the politicians and egghead editorialists had

spun their wheels about what went wrong in 2008 I was in a heck of a lot of trouble. I found some slow-moving lawyers and set about "defending" myself but mainly stalling for time. The Loan Barn was indefensible—*predatory lending* and *fraudulent underwriting practices* were words being thrown around at the time—but I knew something all the Washington idiots didn't know. I knew that places like California and Florida got so excited by future money that they would not be willing to give it up. They were, and are, so addicted to future money that they can't give it up. Like any drug addiction, it would take a concentrated twelve-step program to cure Californians—heck, the whole country—of their addiction to future money. But in 2009 the country was at an all-time low. Every day a new commentator would come on TV with new gloom-and-doom scenarios. A lot of finger waving at consumers and Wall Street bankers and brokers. The home lenders took the brunt of the blame, and frankly we deserved it. Fast Eddy and I once loaned a five-year-old girl a million dollars just because we could! That money was on the books at 20 percent interest. Future money! If you listened to the facts, we wrecked Iceland, we wrecked Italy and we wrecked Greece. We almost took down Europe. It was worse than the Depression. And just like a repentant drunk, we felt really bad . . . for about a day. Then we got thirsty. Out of the shadows like stubborn little jackasses, a breed of News Anchor—I'll call them "News Enablers"—started to whisper, "Hey, the economy isn't so bad." These guys, who called themselves reporters, began suggesting that the losses were overstated and that everyone panicked and that future money was good and real and we could start spending it again. Well, as a student of human nature I saw this coming. We are essentially a country of ham-headed idiots. We love to forget about debt and go water-skiing. I think we all can agree it's better to live in the beautiful fable of future money than live in a boring world like adults where we pay our debts. We are not adults. We are children, and it's just more fun! About three years ago Californians started to buy houses again with money they didn't have—the Loan Barn held on to so many bad loans and toxic assets that it seemed like nothing short of killing everyone involved would clean it up. But that didn't happen. Instead I was able to unload the Loan Barn to a refi company called United American Yankee Liberty First National Mortgage and Security for the tidy sum of forty billion. Now they have all those risky loans on the books and they are valued at ninety billion dollars. The country of Greece has invested its entire pension plan in the company and just can't believe their good fortune!

In the end I didn't need forty billion dollars. I gave most of it away. Some of it went to my favorite charities, Candy Canes for the World and Dolphins for Children. I gave about twenty billion to Iceland because I did feel in a way that I ruined their economy, and gosh darn it if that country just doesn't intrigue the hell out of me. It's a whole land of ice, where ice people live in ice houses. I've never met anyone from Iceland but I would imagine them to be about eight feet tall with long pointy noses and blue skin. I would visit, but no way. I hate the cold.

Today I'm as comfortable as a man of my advanced age

can be. I enjoy cooking and lying out by the pool in the nude. I enjoy that my neighbor Warren Moon and his friends can clearly see me out by the pool in the raw and there's really nothing he can do about it. Occasionally the old gang gets back together to reminisce, sing show tunes and take in a bum fight. Every Christmas I drive by Wes Mantooth's house and throw a brick though his window. He returns the favor every Easter . . . with the same brick! Most mornings Veronica and I can be seen bouncing up and down the coast on our Jet Skis. Most nights we can be seen bouncing up and down by the pool. I still breed labradoodles for anyone who wants them. I'm good friends with Reba McEntire. My long-standing feud with Oscar Mayer meats is over. They were right and I was wrong. My steak knife collection is very famous. I have many honorary degrees but wouldn't say no to a few more. There's nothing so bad on God's green earth that can't be made good by a tall glass of scotch.

# MY FINAL THOUGHTS

Well, that's the end. I know I did a lot of bragging in the beginning about the greatness of this book. Those are just the kinds of straight-faced lies we authors tell you people to get you to read a pile of garbage. Frankly I really thought I had a huge pile of garbage on my hands but I've just read it over and I have to admit something to myself: I'm a great book writer. Will I get the Nobel Prize for this baby? Probably not—maybe an outside chance if a couple of guys die, but probably not. Is it worthy of a Pulitzer? You bet. It really turned out to be a great book that I'm sure will be required reading in colleges for years to come. Oh sure, somewhere down the road it will lose favor with intellectuals and go through a period of neglect, but then some smart professor will find it again and resurrect its greatness and there it will sit on the highest throne with the greatest books of all time. I can accept that fate for this little book.

Before I end it though I thought I'd share a final thought. There's a lot of anger out there. I feel it in the streets. I see it every day on the roadways and in the air. I guess we're a pretty angry bunch of idiots all around. Why is that? Why does mankind hate his brother? Is it as simple as some people have got stuff that other people want? I don't know, but I've got a lot of stuff—Jet Skis and trampolines and football-shaped phones—and sometimes my anger still gets the best of me. I don't think it's just about the stuff. I think, if you really get down to it, we are angry because we are scared. Scared of what? Well, I'm scared of children and elephants. I'm also scared of losing and, heck, I'll say it, I'm scared of dying. When you think about lying in that mud hole and someone shoveling dirt on you, it makes you angry. You start to think, "I don't have as much as I want! I'm not doing what I want to do! I'm not being who I want to be!" Well, it takes courage to do what you want and be who you want to be, and it takes courage to admit you're afraid. I'm afraid all the time. It's hard to say it but I'm afraid right now, afraid an elephant is going to come crashing into my den and crush me. It's a very real fear. The way I deal with it is by staying classy. That's the best medicine of all. If you're busy going about doing what you want to do and being who you want to be, unafraid of what everyone else thinks, you'll be classy too. Sure, the other guy has a flying car and a camera in his watch, but you can have something better. You can have class. Stay classy, America. You know I will.

*Ron Burgundy*

One other thing: The last time I wore a swimsuit while swimming was June 8, 1976. Had that in my notes and it didn't fit anywhere in the book, so I just added it on. Stay classy.

# PHOTOGRAPHY CREDITS

*(In order of appearance)*